To David

Hi guys, Jimmy thought you might like this book

Love, Bart

The Quest for Alpha

The Quest for Alpha

The Holy Grail of Investing

Larry E. Swedroe

WILEY

John Wiley & Sons, Inc.

Published by John Wiley & Sons, Inc., Hoboken, New Jersey.

Published simultaneously in Canada.

For general information on our other products and services or for technical support, please contact our Customer Care Department within the United States at (800) 762-2974, outside the United States at (317) 572-3993 or fax (317) 572-4002.

Wiley also publishes its books in a variety of electronic formats. Some content that appears in print may not be available in electronic books. For more information about Wiley products, visit our web site at www.wiley.com.

Library of Congress Cataloging-in-Publication Data:

Swedroe, Larry E.
   The quest for alpha : the holy grail of investing / Larry E. Swedroe.
      p.   cm.
   Includes bibliographical references and index.
   ISBN 978-0-470-92654-3 (cloth); 978-1-118-00569-9 (ebk); 978-1-118-00570-5 (ebk); 978-1-118-00568-2 (ebk)
      1. Investments. 2. Investment analysis. 3. Portfolio management.   I. Title.
HG4527.S944 2011
332.6—dc22

2010034716

Printed in the United States of America
10 9 8 7 6 5 4

*This book is dedicated to my three daughters,
Jodi Rosen, Jennifer Morris, Jacquelyn Swedroe;
my sons-in-law Jay Rosen and Matt Morris;
and my three grandchildren, Jonathan,
Sophie Rosen, and Ruby Jane Morris.
You have all brought great
joy to my life.*

Contents

Acknowledgments

For all their support and encouragement, I would like to thank the principals of The Buckingham Family of Financial Services: Adam Birenbaum, Ernest Clark, Bob Gellman, Ed Goldberg, Mont Levy, Steve Lourie, Vladimir Masek, Bert Schweizer III, and Brenda Witt.

Too many of my coworkers contributed to list them all. However, I would be remiss if I did not mention the special efforts and contributions of RC Balaban, who edits my blog at www.moneywatch.bnet.com and Vladimir Masek, from whom I have learned a great deal about the science of investing. The usual caveat of any errors being my own certainly applies.

I also thank my agent Sam Fleischman for all his efforts over the years and for getting me started as an author. I am forever grateful for his support and friendship.

I especially thank my wife, Mona, the love of my life, for her tremendous encouragement and understanding during the lost weekends and many nights I sat at the computer well into the early morning hours. She has always provided whatever support was needed—and then some. Walking through life with her has truly been a gracious experience.

Introduction

The most difficult subjects can be explained to the most slow-witted man if he has not formed any idea of them already; but the simplest thing cannot be made clear to the most intelligent man if he is firmly persuaded that he knows already, without a shadow of a doubt, what is laid before him.
—LEO TOLSTOY

I am the director of research and a principal of The Buckingham Family of Financial Services. All of us at Buckingham are particularly proud of two things. The first is that we provide a fiduciary standard of care, requiring us to put the interests of our clients ahead of our own. You could say that we "eat our own cooking," investing our own personal assets in the same vehicles we recommend to our clients. The second is that our advice is based on the science of investing, or evidence-based investing, not our opinions.

This book presents the evidence from studies published in peer-reviewed academic journals. In addition, you will read the advice of legendary investors such as Benjamin Graham (co-author of *Security Analysis*), Peter Lynch (who manged Fidelity's Magellan Fund), and Warren Buffett (CEO of Berkshire Hathaway). And you will be amazed at some of the admissions of industry practitioners and members of the financial media.

The Holy Grail

According to Christian mythology, the Holy Grail was the dish, plate, or cup used by Jesus at the Last Supper, and said to possess miraculous powers. Legend has it that the Grail was sent to Great Britain, where several guardians keep it safe. The search for the Holy Grail is an important part of the legends of King Arthur and his court, with Percival, one of the Knights of the Round Table, and Galahad, Lancelot's son, playing the major roles.

The financial equivalent of the quest for the Holy Grail is the quest for the money managers who *will* deliver alpha— returns above the appropriate risk-adjusted benchmark. Our journey together on this quest is really a tale of two competing theories about how markets work and which investment strategy is most likely to allow you to achieve your financial goals.

The first theory is based on the conventional wisdom that the markets are inefficient. If markets are inefficient, smart people working diligently can discover pricing errors the market makes. They can discover which stocks are undervalued (Intel is trading at 20 but is really worth 30) and buy them.

And they can discover which stocks are overvalued (IBM is trading at 30 but is really worth 20) and avoid them; or, if they are aggressive, they can sell them short (borrow IBM stock, sell it at 30, then buy it back at 20 when the market corrects its error). That is called the art of stock selection.

In addition, smart people can also anticipate when the bull is going to enter the arena. They will recommend increasing your allocation to stocks ahead of the anticipated rally. They can also anticipate when the bear is going to emerge from hibernation and will recommend lowering your equity allocation ahead of that event. This is called the art of market timing.

Stock selection and market timing combine to form the art of active management. And active management is the conventional wisdom—ideas that are so accepted by the general public that they mostly go unchallenged.

If markets are inefficient, the winning strategy is to identify the managers with the ability to exploit the market's inefficiencies. The way to do that is to study past performance. You then hire the managers who have demonstrated a persistent ability to generate alpha.

There is a competing theory based on about 60 years of academic research. The body of work is called Modern Portfolio Theory (MPT). Its premise is that markets are highly efficient—the market price of a security is the best estimate of the right price. *(Otherwise, the market would clear at a different price.)* If markets are highly efficient, efforts to outperform are unlikely to prove productive after the expenses of the efforts. If that is true, the winning strategy is to focus on the following: asset allocation, fund construction, costs, tax efficiency, and the building of globally diversified portfolios that minimize, if not eliminate, the taking of idiosyncratic, and therefore uncompensated, risks.

The debate about which theory is right and which strategy is the one most likely to produce the best results is the financial equivalent of the popular debates among the drinkers of Miller Lite of "Tastes great! Less filling!" And, like that debate, it is unlikely to end. There is one important difference between the debates. In the case of Miller Lite, there may not be a right answer. However, investors need to know if there is a right answer to the question of which theory and strategy is the right one. The problem is how to know which is correct. Are markets efficient or inefficient?

Despite the fact money is probably the third most important thing in our lives (not money itself, but what money provides) after our family and our health, our education system has totally failed to equip investors with the knowledge required to determine the answer to our question. Unless you have an MBA in finance, it is likely that you have never taken even a single course in capital markets theory. That is why I wrote this book—to provide you with the information that will lead you to the answer.

The Quest Begins

We begin our quest by asking the question: are markets inefficient? If they are inefficient, we should see evidence of the persistent ability to outperform risk-adjusted benchmarks. It is important that any persistence be greater than randomly expected. Imagine the following scenario: There are 10,000 individuals gathered to participate in a coin-tossing contest. A coin will be tossed, and contestants must guess whether it will come up heads or tails. Anyone who correctly guesses the outcome of 10 consecutive tosses will be declared a winner and will receive the coveted title of "coin-tossing guru." According to statistics, we can *expect* after the first toss that 5,000 participants have guessed right and 5,000 have guessed wrong. After the second round, the remaining participants will be expected to be 2,500, and so on. After 10 repetitions we would *expect* to have 10 remaining participants who would have guessed correctly all 10 times and earned their guru status. (Note that the actual number will likely be different from the expected.) What probability would you attach to the likelihood that those 10 gurus would win the next coin-toss competition? Would you bet on them winning? The answers are obvious. Similarly, if there are 10,000 money managers (or monkeys throwing darts at a stock table as a way to pick stocks), we should randomly expect the same type of outcome in terms of performance. In order to show that markets are inefficient, we need to see evidence of persistent outperformance *beyond the randomly expected*. Otherwise, we cannot differentiate skill from luck.

The good news is that it is easy to identify the managers and funds that have outperformed. All you need is a database. Since databases are readily available, we are left with the question: is the past prologue? We will answer that question by examining the evidence from academic studies on:

- Mutual funds
- Pension plans
- Hedge funds
- Private equity/venture capital
- Individual investors
- Behavioral finance

We begin our survey of the academic literature with the evidence on the performance of actively managed mutual funds.

Chapter 1

Mutual Funds: The Evidence

There are many studies on the performance of actively managed equity mutual funds. They provide evidence that is both consistent and overwhelming. For example, a 2002 study by Mark Carhart and three colleagues analyzed the performance of 2,071 equity funds for the period 1962–1995. They found that the average actively managed fund underperformed its appropriate passive benchmark on a pretax basis by about 1.8 percent per annum.[1] This study built on the work of an earlier Carhart paper, "On Persistence in Mutual Fund Performance." Among its conclusions were:

- There was no persistence in performance beyond what would be randomly expected—the past performance of active managers is a poor predictor of their future performance.

- Expenses both reduce returns on a one-for-one basis and explain much of the persistent long-term underperformance of mutual funds.
- Turnover reduces pretax returns by almost 1 percent of the value of the trade.

Carhart's conclusion: "While the popular press will no doubt continue to glamorize the best-performing mutual-fund managers, the mundane explanations of strategy [asset-class allocation, not individual stock selection] and investment costs account for almost all of the important predictability in mutual fund returns."[2]

Keep in mind that Carhart's findings are all pretax. After taxes, the results would have been worse because of the greater turnover incurred by actively managed funds.

When You Wish upon a Morningstar

One of the most common investment strategies employed by individual investors is to buy the mutual funds that are highly rated by Morningstar. Morningstar itself provided us with evidence on how successful a strategy that is.

The November 2009 issue of Morningstar's *FundInvestor* provided the following evidence on its five-star funds:

- The 2004 class of five-star domestic funds had a five-year rating of just 3.2, just slightly above average. And, as we have seen, the average fund has underperformed its risk-adjusted benchmark by close to 2 percent.
- The 2005 group of five-star funds had a three-year rating of just 3.1.
- The 2006 group had a three-year rating of just 2.9.

The paper "Mutual Fund Ratings and Future Performance" from the Vanguard Institute provides further evidence on the ability of star ratings to predict the future.[3]

Authors Christopher B. Philips and Francis M. Kinniry Jr. examined the excess returns over the three-year period following a given rating. They chose the three-year period because Morningstar requires at least three years of performance data to generate a rating and investment committees typically use a three-year window to evaluate the performance of their portfolio managers. The period covered was June 30, 1992 through August 31, 2009. The following is a summary of their findings:

- Thirty-nine percent of funds with five-star ratings outperformed their style benchmarks for the 36 months following the rating, while 46 percent of one-star funds did so.
- Most of the star-rating groups produced negative excess returns in the succeeding three years. Even worse, the four- and five-star figures were more negative than those of lower-rated groups.

Philips and Kinniry concluded: "Higher ratings in no way ensured that an investor would increase his or her odds of outperforming a style benchmark in subsequent years."

In fact, they found that "5-star funds showed the lowest probability of maintaining their rating, confirming that sustainable outperformance is difficult. This means that investors who focus on investing only in highly rated funds may find themselves continuously buying and selling funds as ratings change. Such turnover could lead to higher costs and lower returns as investors are continuously chasing yesterday's winner."

The bottom line is that using Morningstar's ratings system is like driving forward while looking through the rearview mirror. The system does a great job of "predicting" the past.

The Vanguard Institute paper also addressed one of the questions I am frequently asked: "If index funds are so good, why do many of them carry three-star (average) ratings?" The authors explain that "the natural distribution of the actively managed fund universe around a benchmark (the index) dictates that an appropriately constructed and managed index fund should fall somewhere near the center of that distribution." (It is important to note that it will fall to the right of the center of distribution due to lower costs.)

Think of it this way: A sprinter in a 100-yard dash might be able to overcome wearing a two-pound weight on each ankle, but the odds of doing so decrease with the length of the race. And the odds of winning a marathon with that handicap are close to zero. Thus, it is over longer periods that cost advantages of passively managed funds have a greater influence on the distribution of relative performance.

Focus Funds

One often-heard excuse for the failure of the typical mutual fund is they are "overdiversified"—by owning so many stocks, the value of the manager's best ideas are diluted. Warren Buffett seems to agree with that hypothesis. Here is what he had to say about diversification: "Wide diversification is only required when investors do not understand what they are doing."[4]

The mutual fund industry's solution (or sales pitch) to what Buffett called "di-worse-si-fying" portfolios is to create "focus" funds—funds that concentrate holdings in the manager's best ideas. While most mutual funds hold well over 100 stocks, the typical focus fund will hold 40 or less. There are even funds that hire several submanagers for just their single best pick.

The question for investors is: does concentration of risk improve returns? Travis Sapp (associate professor of finance, Iowa State University) and Xuemin (Sterling) Yan (associate professor of finance, University of Missouri, Columbia) sought the answer to that question in their 2008 study "Security

Concentrations and Active Fund Management: Do Focused Funds Offer Superior Performance?"[5] Their database covered the period from 1984 through 2002 and contained 2,278 funds comprising 16,399 fund-years. The study excluded funds with less than 12 holdings, as well as those with less than $1 million in assets. The following summarizes their findings:

- There was no evidence that focus funds outperform diversified funds. In fact, after controlling for other fund characteristics, funds with a large number of holdings significantly outperformed funds with a small number of holdings both before and after expenses—fund performance was positively, not negatively, correlated to the number of securities in the portfolio.
- The quintile of funds with the fewest holdings realized an economically and statistically significant annual three-factor alpha of negative 1.44 percent.
- At the one-year horizon, the buys of focus funds *underperformed* their sells by 0.3 percent.
- Focus funds have significantly higher return volatility and tracking error to benchmarks. Thus, investors were taking greater risk while earning lower returns.
- Focus funds held considerably larger cash positions: 12.8 percent versus 7.8 percent for diversified funds. Cash acts as a drag on returns for equity funds.
- The attrition rate of focus funds is higher than for diversified funds.

One explanation for the underperformance of focus funds is that the larger the ownership stake in a stock becomes, the greater the trading costs—the fund cannot react quickly to new information without incurring significant trading costs. As the authors noted, "Even if managers of focused funds have better stock-picking ability, their funds might not perform better than diversified funds because of liquidity problems." Once trading costs are added to the burden of their relatively high operating expense ratios, achieving a positive risk-adjusted alpha becomes difficult. This issue is discussed further in Chapter 7.

Another explanation for the failure of focus funds is that while the market may not be perfectly efficient, it is sufficiently efficient that *after expenses* it is difficult to exploit any pricing errors.

The evidence on bond mutual funds is just as compelling.

Active Management of Bond Funds

The following are the results of just two of the many studies that could be cited on the attempts of active management to exploit market inefficiencies in the fixed income markets. Christopher R. Blake (professor of finance, Fordham University, Graduate School of Business Administration), Edwin J. Elton (professor of finance, NYU, Stern School of Business,), and Martin J. Gruber's (professor of finance, NYU, Stern School of Business) 1993 study, "The Performance of Bond Mutual Funds," covered as many as 361 bond funds and showed that the average actively managed bond fund underperformed its benchmark index by 0.75 percent to 0.95 percent per annum.[6] A 1994 article in *Fortune* magazine reported that only 16 percent of 800 fixed income funds beat their relevant benchmark over the 10-year period covered.[7]

Of course, being a loser's game does not mean there are not some winners. The fact that there are winners allows investors to hope that they can identify the few winners ahead of time. The evidence from a study by Marlena I. Lee of Dimensional Fund Advisors suggests otherwise.

Lee studied the performance of 2,353 bond funds over the period 1991–2008, which included investment-grade, high-yield, and government bond funds. The following is a summary of her findings:[8]

- Actively managed bond funds underperformed by an amount roughly equal to fees.
- Expense ratios were a good predictor of performance.
- Good past performance did not predict good future performance. There was no evidence of positive after-cost expected alphas, even in the top percentile of funds.
- Underperformance of loser funds persisted for several years. Most of the persistence in loser returns could be attributed to fees.
- Collectively, investors in active bond funds lose about 90 basis points per year, or about $1.4 billion in 2008, in underperformance.

Lee concluded: "Although some investors may believe that the higher fees associated with active management are compensation for return-enhancing abilities, the data do not show this."

She added: "These results indicate the unlikelihood that investors can profit from investing in funds with good past performance, but they may be able to shield themselves from poor risk-adjusted returns by avoiding funds with poor past performance."

Other studies on the subject, including those on municipal bond funds, all reach the same conclusions:

- Past performance cannot be used to predict future performance.
- Actively managed funds do not, on average, provide value added in terms of returns.
- The major cause of underperformance is expenses—there is a consistent one-for-one negative relationship between expense ratios and net returns.

The results of a 2004 study by Morningstar demonstrated both the importance of costs and that past performance of actively managed funds is a poor predictor of future performance.

It tested funds with strong performance and high costs against those with poor past performance with low costs. "Sure enough, those with low costs outperformed in the following period."[9]

Why did all these studies come to the conclusion that bond fund managers charge Georgia O'Keeffe prices and deliver paint-by-numbers results? The Efficient Market Hypothesis (EMH) provides the answer: the market's efficiency prevents active managers from persistently exploiting any mispricing. And as difficult as it is for active managers to add value when it comes to equity investing, it is much harder for them to add value in fixed income investing. Let's see why this is true.

First, with U.S. Treasury debt, all bonds of the same maturity will provide the same return—there is no ability to add value via security selection. If we restrict holdings to the highest investment grades, there is an extremely limited ability to add value via security selection—while the stocks of two companies with AAA bond ratings can perform quite differently, their bonds of similar maturity will likely produce very similar results (because credit risk is low). The higher the credit rating, the more likely it is that bonds of the same rating will produce similar returns.

That leaves interest rate forecasting as the only way an active manager might add value in any significant way. And there is no evidence of any persistent ability to forecast interest rates. (The value of economic forecasts in general is discussed in Chapter 7.)

We turn now to one reason why past performance of active managers should not be relied on as a predictor of future performance.

Skill versus Luck

Trying to discern the lucky from the skilled can be very difficult in many walks of life. For example, every time there is a professional sports draft, the debate flares up whether the evaluation of college (or even high school) athletes is an exercise in skill or luck.

For example, the Houston Rockets had the first pick in the 1984 NBA draft. They chose Hakeem Olajuwon. With the second pick, the Portland Trail Blazers selected Sam Bowie instead of Michael Jordan. While Bowie went on to an uneventful and injury-plagued career, Jordan led the Chicago Bulls to six championships and is considered by many to be the greatest player ever. Were the Blazers unskilled or just unlucky? The point is that sometimes it is very difficult to discern luck from skill. This difficulty extends to the evaluation of active mutual fund managers.

Bradford Cornell, professor of financial economics at the California Institute of Technology, contributed to the literature with his 2009 study, "Luck, Skill and Investment Performance."[10] Cornell noted: "Successful investing, like most activities in life, is based on a combination of skill and serendipity. Distinguishing between the two is critical for forward-looking decision-making because skill is relatively permanent while serendipity, or luck, by definition is not. An investment manager who is skillful this year presumably will be skillful next year. An investment manager who was lucky this year is no more likely to be lucky next year than any other manager. The problem is that skill and luck are not independently observable."

Since skill and luck are not directly observable, we are left with observing performance. However, we can apply standard statistical analysis to help differentiate the two—which is what Cornell did.

He used Morningstar's 2004 database of mutual fund performance to analyze a homogeneous sample of 1,034 funds that invest in large-cap value stocks. Cornell's findings are consistent with the previous research. The great majority (92 percent) of the cross-sectional variation in fund performance is due to random noise. This result demonstrates that "most of the annual variation in performance is due to luck, not skill." He concluded: "The analysis also provides further support for the view that annual rankings of fund performance provide almost no information regarding management skill."

Professors Eugene F. Fama (professor of finance, University of Chicago, Booth School of Business) and Kenneth R. French (professor of finance, Dartmouth College, Tuck School of Business) also studied this issue in their March 2009 paper, "Luck versus Skill in the Cross Section of Mutual Fund Alpha Estimates." The two academics looked at mutual fund data from the Center for Research in Security Prices. Using statistical analysis, Fama and French found that active managers as a group have not added any value over appropriate passive benchmarks. They concluded: "For (active) fund investors the simulation results are disheartening."

They did concede that the results looked better when looking at gross returns—the returns without the expense ratio included. However, gross returns are irrelevant to investors unless they can find an active manager willing to work for free. The bottom line is that Fama and French found no evidence of fund managers with skill sufficient to cover costs.[11]

It is important to note that the evidence on both the aggregate underperformance and the lack of persistent outperformance beyond the randomly expected has been found regardless of the asset class. So the argument that active management wins in "inefficient" asset classes like small caps or emerging markets is simply a myth. As you will see, the same underperformance has been found whether the markets are rising or falling.

The 2009 Spring/Summer issue of *Vanguard Investment Perspectives* provides us with evidence on the performance of actively managed equity funds during bear markets. Vanguard's study covered the period 1970–2008 and examined the returns of active funds during the seven periods when the Dow Jones Wilshire 5000 Index fell at least 10 percent and the six periods when the MSCI EAFE Index fell by at least that amount. Despite acknowledging survivorship bias (poorly performing funds disappear and are not accounted for), Vanguard found:

- It didn't matter whether an active manager was operating in a bear market, a bull market that precedes or follows it, or across longer-term cycles, the costs of security selection and market timing proved a difficult hurdle to overcome.
- "Success" can be explained at least in part by style exposures. For example, during the bear market of September 2000–March 2003, the Russell 1000 Value Index fell just 21 percent, while the U.S. total market lost more than 42 percent. Once active funds were compared to their style benchmarks, there was no consistent pattern of outperformance. Past success in overcoming this hurdle didn't ensure future success. "The degree of attrition among winners from one period to the next indicates that successfully navigating one or even two bear markets might be more strongly linked to simple luck than to skill."

Vanguard concluded: "We find little evidence to support the purported benefits of active management during periods of market stress."

Vanguard's conclusion is confirmed by Standard & Poor's finding in its *2008 Indices vs. Active Scorecard*. S&P concluded: "The belief that bear markets favor active management is a myth. A majority of active funds in eight of the nine domestic equity style boxes were outperformed by indices in the negative markets of 2008. The bear market of 2000 to 2002 showed similar outcomes."

As the evidence demonstrates, the belief that active managers are likely to protect you from bear markets is just another myth perpetuated by Wall Street.

Who Cares about the Average Fund?

Whenever I present this type of evidence, the typical response from skeptics goes something like: "Who cares about the average fund? I invest only in the best funds, the ones with great track records." The problem with this line of thinking is that all the studies on this subject have found no persistent outperformance beyond the randomly expected—the past is not prologue when it comes to mutual fund returns. And, as you will see, even a long record of persistent outperformance has little value.

With Active Managers, How Long Is Long Enough?

Streaks randomly occur with much greater frequency than people believe. For example, the odds of flipping a coin 20 times and getting either four heads or four tails in a row are 50 percent. Because people underestimate the frequency of streaks, they tend to assign far too much meaning to events that are highly likely to be random occurrences. One study even demonstrated that a "hot hand" in basketball was likely to be nothing more than a random event. A statistician following a basketball team around for an entire season found that the odds of a career 50 percent shooter hitting the next shot were 50 percent, even if this player had just hit five shots in a row. The hot hand, at least for basketball, is a myth.[12]

Erroneously overreacting to what are random events can lead to not only poor coaching decisions but poor investment decisions as well. Hopefully, the following evidence will convince you that the Securities and Exchange Commission's (SEC's) required disclaimer that past performance doesn't guarantee future results is far too weak. It should read: *Past performance is not indicative of future results.* We begin with perhaps the best example of why past is not prologue when it comes to the performance of active managers.

The 44 Wall Street Fund

Most investors would be surprised to learn that Peter Lynch's Magellan Fund was not the top-ranked fund of the 1970s. Thanks to its now long-forgotten manager David Baker, the 44 Wall Street Fund generated even greater returns than Peter Lynch's Magellan Fund in the 1970s and ranked as the top-performing diversified U.S. stock fund of the decade. Surely, 10 years of the best performance in an entire industry could not be the result of luck. Or could it? How were investors rewarded for believing that past performance of active managers is prologue?

While the S&P 500 Index returned 17.6 percent per year—each $1 invested grew to over $5—the 44 Wall Street Fund ranked as the single worst-performing fund in the 1980s, losing 73 percent—turning each $1 invested into just 27 cents. The fund did so poorly that it was merged into the Cumberland Growth Fund in April 1993, which was then merged into the Matterhorn Growth Fund in April 1996.

We next consider the case of a fund that accomplished what even Lynch never did—beating the S&P 500 11 years in a row.

The Lindner Large-Cap Fund

For each of the 11 years 1974–1984, the Lindner Large-Cap Fund outperformed the S&P 500 Index. However, over the next 18 years, the S&P 500 Index returned 12.6 percent per annum. Believers in past performance as a prologue to future performance were rewarded for their faith in the Lindner Large-Cap Fund with returns of just 4.1 percent, an underperformance of 8.5 percent per year for 18 years. The Lindner fund was finally put out of its misery when it was purchased by the Hennessy Funds in October 2003 and eventually merged into the Hennessy Total Return Fund.

Then there is the case of Bill Miller, who managed to beat the S&P 500 Index 15 years in a row. Surely that long a streak of excellence could be relied on. Clearly, it could not have been the result of luck. Or could it?

The Legg Mason Value Trust Fund

By the end of 2005, Bill Miller's streak of outperforming the S&P 500 Index had reached 15 years. Unfortunately for investors, that streak was broken in 2006 when the fund underperformed the S&P 500 Index by about 10 percent. His 2007 performance was even worse, underperforming the S&P 500 Index by 12 percent. And 2008 was even more miserable, as the fund underperformed that benchmark by 18 percent. Miller finally reversed that performance in 2009, as his fund beat the S&P 500 Index by 14 percent.

There is one last case to present. Although it is not about a mutual fund, it is a tale about relying on the past performance of active managers.

The Tiger Fund

The Tiger Fund was a hedge fund formed in 1980 by the legendary Julian Robertson with $10 million in capital. The fund had a remarkable run, averaging more than 30 percent a year for the first 18 years. By 1998, it had in excess of $22 billion under management—the vast majority coming from new investments. And it is from this height that it began its fall into oblivion, generating losses of some $10 billion from peak to closing. The irony is that while the fund still showed a return of 25 percent per year over its life, it is estimated that investors in the fund may have actually lost money. The reason is that most of the money came in late, after the great returns had already been earned.

These tales demonstrate that 10, 11, 15, or even 18 years of outperformance are not sufficient to draw reliable conclusions.

What always surprises me is that while people concerned about their personal health will heed the surgeon general's warning about the dangers of cigarettes, they will ignore the SEC warning that relying on past performance of money managers is dangerous to your financial health.

The body of evidence on past performance being a reliable predictor of future performance of money managers has led many to the conclusion that investing in actively managed funds is a loser's game. Pay close attention to the conclusions drawn by some of our most respected investment managers and financial economists.

Advice from Professional Investors and Academics

Burton Malkiel is a professor of economics at Princeton University. He has also served as a member of the Council of Economic Advisors, president of the American Finance Association, and dean of the Yale School of Management. He was also on the board of the Vanguard Group for 28 years. Malkiel is probably best known as the author of the book *A Random Walk Down Wall Street,* in which he had this to say about past performance of mutual fund managers:

> I have become increasingly convinced that the past records of mutual fund managers are essentially worthless in predicting future success. The few examples of consistently superior performance occur no more frequently than can be expected by chance.[13]

David F. Swensen has been the chief investment officer of the Yale Endowment Fund since 1985. He is one of the most respected investment managers in the world. He is also the author of *Pioneering Portfolio Management* and *Unconventional Success*. Swensen had this to say about mutual funds fees and performance:

> Overwhelmingly, mutual funds extract enormous sums from investors in exchange for providing a shocking disservice. That is, mutual funds charge their investors big fees and usually fail to deliver returns that beat the market.[14]

In his book *Unconventional Success*, Swensen provided this advice for investors:

> Compelling data show that nearly certain disappointment awaits the mutual-fund shareholder who hopes to generate market-beating returns.[15]

John Bogle is the founder and former chairman of the Vanguard Group. In 1999, *Fortune* named him one of the investment industry's four "Giants of the 20th Century." In 2004, *Time* named him one of the world's 100 most powerful and influential people. The same year, he also received *Institutional Investor*'s Lifetime Achievement Award.

He is the author of seven books on investing. "Saint Jack," as he is known because of his tireless crusading efforts on behalf of individual investors, is one of the most respected people in the world of finance. In his book *Common Sense on Mutual Funds*, Bogle had this to say on the ability of investment advisors to identify the money managers that *will* deliver alpha:

> I do not believe that they can identify, *in advance*, the top-performing managers—no one can!—and, I'd avoid those who claim they can do so.[16]

In his keynote speech at the Personal Finance Conference on January 30, 1999, Bogle advised:

> Make no mistake about it, the record is clear that top-performing funds inevitably lose their edge.

If asked to name the investment professionals they respect the most, it is safe to say that most people would have Warren Buffett at, or near, the top of their list. In the 1993 Berkshire Hathaway Annual Report, Buffett provided this advice:

> By periodically investing in an index fund the know-nothing investor can actually outperform most investment professionals.

Given the sources, the cumulative weight of the advice should be sufficient to convince most people of the futility of trying to identify future outperformers by reviewing past performance. However, we are not yet done. Given the sources, careful attention should be paid to the quotations that follow.

Admissions from Industry Practitioners and the Financial Media

Ralph Wanger was the highly regarded lead manager of the Acorn Fund from its inception in 1977 until his retirement in 2003. During this period, the fund returned 16.3 percent per annum versus just 12.1 percent for the S&P 500 Index. Wanger is also the author of the book *A Zebra in Lion Country*. In his book, he made this startling admission:

> For professional investors like myself, a sense of humor is essential for another reason. We are very aware that we are competing not only against the market averages but also against one another. It's an intense rivalry. We are each claiming, "The stocks in my fund

today will perform better than what you own in your fund." That implies we think we can predict the future, which is the occupation of charlatans. If you believe you or anyone else has a system that can predict the future of the stock market, the joke is on you.[17]

Bill Miller, the highly regarded manager of the Legg Mason Value Trust Fund, said:

The S&P 500 is a wonderful thing to put your money in. If somebody said, "I've got a fund here with a really low cost, that's tax efficient, with a 15- to 20-year record of beating almost everybody," why wouldn't you own it?[18]

Douglas Dial was the manager of the CREF Stock Account, one of the largest funds in the world, when he commented:

Indexing is a marvelous technique. I wasn't a true believer. I was just an ignoramus. Now I am a convert. Indexing is an extraordinary sophisticated thing to do. . . . If people want excitement, they should go to the racetrack or play the lottery.[19]

The following is important because it comes from Morningstar, the seller of a service that rates mutual funds:

For starters, expense ratios are the best predictors of performance—way better than historical returns. It's tempting to look at strong past performance and assume a fund can repeat its success, but there's no guarantee it will. In fact, we've found that you'd be better off randomly picking a fund with expenses in the cheapest quartile and past returns in the worst quartile than a fund with returns in the top quartile and expenses in the highest quartile. In addition, for the investor, there isn't much logic to costs. Higher expenses don't get you better management. If it did you'd expect higher-cost funds to outperform their lower-cost peers—when in fact just the opposite has happened.[20]

The following quotations are important because of their source: the financial media and publications that anoint the latest hot manager as a guru and tout the hot funds you just have to own.

The first is from an article by *BusinessWeek* reporter Robert Barker. In his December 17, 2001, column, "It's Tough to Find Fund Whizzes," Barker observed:

> If picking stocks is a random walk down Wall Street, as Princeton economist Burton Malkiel famously put it, then picking mutual funds is an obstacle course through Hell's Kitchen.

The next quotations are from *Fortune*:

> Despite the solemn import that fund companies attribute to past performance, there is no evidence that the 4 percent who beat the index owe their record to anything other than random statistical variation.[21]

> We have learned that past investment records make lousy crystal balls.[22]

> Despite volumes of research attesting to the meaninglessness of past returns, most investors (and personal finance magazines) seek tomorrow's winners among yesterday's. Forget it.[23]

> That sort of skepticism about past returns is crucial. The truth is, as much as you may wish you could know which funds will be hot, you can't—and neither can the legions of advisers and publications that claim they can. That's why building a portfolio around index funds isn't really settling for average (or a little better). It's just refusing to believe in magic.[24]

John Rekenthaler is the vice president of research and product development at Morningstar, a firm best known for its mutual fund ratings service. Here is what he had to say about the ability to identify future alpha:

> "We should have more answers," he said, while noting there is "surprisingly little" that we can say for sure about how to find topnotch stock funds.[25]

Commenting on whether investors should pay attention to mutual fund advertisements, Rekenthaler had this to say:

> To be fair, I don't think that you'd want to pay much attention to Morningstar's star ratings either.[26]

Don Phillips is managing director of Morningstar. Read carefully his admission in an interview with the *Wall Street Journal*:

> The very likely takeaway may be that it's too hard to pick managers— these great mythic figures don't walk the earth.[27]

Jason Zweig is the personal finance columnist for the *Wall Street Journal*. He is also the author of *Your Money and Your Brain* and the coauthor of the updated version of Benjamin Graham's classic, *The Intelligent Investor*. Here is what Zweig had to say about the chances of identifying future alpha generators:

> Your chances of selecting the top funds of the future are about as high as the odds that Bigfoot and the Abominable Snowman will both show up in pink ballet slippers at your next cocktail party.[28]

Jonathan Clements was the personal finance columnist for the *Wall Street Journal* when he warned investors:

> Santa Claus and the Easter Bunny should take a few pointers from the mutual fund industry [and its fund managers]. All three are trying to pull off elaborate hoaxes. But while Santa and the bunny suffer the derision of eight-year-olds everywhere, actively managed stock funds still have an ardent following among otherwise clear-thinking adults. This continued loyalty amazes me. Reams of statistics prove that most of the fund industry's stock pickers fail to beat the market.[29]

The following "shaggy dog" story is a fitting conclusion to this chapter. Lost on a country road, a man notices a farmer tending his sheep and decides to ask for directions. After thanking the farmer for the directions, he tells the farmer he has an unusual talent. He says: "If I can guess exactly how many sheep you have on that hill, can I take one with me?" Thinking there was no way anyone could guess exactly how many sheep he tended, the farmer agrees. The man scans the hill quickly and says 2,376. Shocked, the farmer says: "That's amazing. I am a man of my word. Go ahead and pick out a sheep." The man marches up the hill and carries back his choice. The farmer says: "Before you leave, I would like a chance to win back my animal. I bet I can guess what you do for a living." Of course, the man accepts this challenge. The farmer says: "You're a manager of an actively managed fund." Stunned, the man says: "How did you know that?" The farmer responded: "Out of 2,376 sheep, only an active manager could pick out the one dog."

We now turn to the evidence on pension plans.

Chapter 2

Pension Plans: The Evidence

I t seems logical to believe that if anyone could beat the market, it would be the pension plans of U.S. companies. Why is this a good assumption? First, pension plans control large sums of money, giving them access to the best and brightest portfolio managers, each clamoring to manage the billions of dollars in these plans (and earn large fees). Pension plans can also invest with managers that most individuals don't have access to because they don't have sufficient assets to meet the minimums of these superstars.

Second, it is not even remotely possible that these pension plans ever hired a manager who did not have a track record of outperforming their benchmarks, or at the very least matching them. Certainly, they would never hire a manager with a record of underperformance.

Third, it is also safe to say that they never hired a manager who did not make a great presentation, explaining why the manager had succeeded and why she would continue to succeed. Surely, the case presented was a convincing one.

Fourth, many of these pension plans, if not the majority, hire professional consultants such as Frank Russell, SEI, and Goldman Sachs to help them perform due diligence in interviewing, screening, and ultimately selecting the very best. For example, Frank Russell boasted that it held more than 5,200 meetings with money managers in 2009. And you can be sure that these consultants have thought of every conceivable screen to find the best fund managers. Surely, they have considered not only performance records, but also such factors as management tenure, depth of staff, consistency of performance (to make sure that a long-term record is not the result of one or two lucky years), performance in bear markets, consistency of implementation of strategy, turnover, costs, and so on. It is unlikely that there is something you or your financial adviser would think of that they had not already considered.

Fifth, as individuals, it is rare that we would have the luxury of being able to personally interview money managers and perform as thorough a due diligence as do these consultants. And we generally don't have professionals helping us to avoid mistakes in the process.

Sixth, the fees they pay for active management are much lower than the fees individual investors pay.

So how has the performance of pension plans stacked up against risk-adjusted benchmarks? The 2007 paper "The Performance of U.S. Pension Plans" sought the answer to that question. The study covered 716 defined benefit plans (1992–2004) and 238 defined contribution plans (1997–2004). The authors found that their returns relative to benchmarks were close to zero. They also found there was no persistence in pension plan performance—the same outcome we saw with mutual funds. Despite the conventional wisdom, past performance is not a reliable predictor of future performance. Importantly, the authors also found neither fund size, degree of outsourcing, nor company stock holdings were factors driving performance. This finding refutes the claim that large pension plans are handicapped by their size. Small plans did no better. Importantly, the authors concluded: "We show striking similarities in net performance patterns over time, which makes skill differences highly unlikely."[1]

The authors also studied the performance of mutual funds, adding to our body of evidence on them. As you should expect, the news for individual investors is even worse. While pension plans failed to outperform market benchmarks, on a risk-adjusted basis mutual funds underperformed pension plans by about 2 percent per annum. Pension plans are able to use their size (negotiating power) to minimize costs and reduce the risks of any conflicts of interests between the fund managers and the investors. The authors attributed the underperformance to the incremental costs incurred by mutual fund investors.

Counterproductive Activity

A study by Amit Goyal (associate professor of finance, Emory University) and Sunil Wahal (professor of finance, Arizona State University) provides us with further evidence on the inability of plan sponsors to identify investment management firms that will outperform the market *after* they are hired. Goyal and Wahal examined the selection and termination of investment management firms by plan sponsors (public and corporate pension plans, union pension plans, foundations, and endowments). They built a dataset of the hiring and firing decisions of approximately 3,400 plan sponsors from 1994 to

2003. The data represented the allocation of over $627 billion in mandates. The following is a summary of their findings:[2]

- Plan sponsors hire investment managers after large positive excess returns up to three years prior to hiring.
- The return-chasing behavior does not deliver positive excess returns thereafter.
- Posthiring excess returns are indistinguishable from zero.
- Plan sponsors terminate investment managers after underperformance, but the excess returns of these managers after being fired are frequently positive.
- If plan sponsors had stayed with the fired investment managers, their returns would have been larger than those actually delivered by the newly hired managers.

It is important to note that the above results did not include any of the trading costs that would have accompanied transitioning a portfolio from one manager's holdings to the holdings preferred by the new manager. The bottom line: all of the activity was counterproductive.

Another study of pension fund managers found the same results. T. Daniel Coggin and Charles A. Trzcinka studied the performance of 292 pension plans with 12 quarters of data up to the second quarter of 1993.[3] The following summarizes their findings:

- It is very difficult to find investment managers who consistently add value relative to appropriate benchmarks.
- There was no correlation found between relative performance in one period and future periods.
- There was no evidence that the number of managers beating their benchmarks was greater than pure chance.

The authors concluded: "Those who rely solely on historical style alphas to predict future style alphas are likely to be disappointed."

The Value of Consultants

Table 2.1 compares the returns of the passive asset class funds for the 13-year period 1997–2009 of Dimensional Fund Advisors (DFA) to those of the comparable funds of two of the largest institutional money managers/consultants in the world, SEI and Frank Russell. As you can see, the actively managed funds of SEI and Russell underperformed the passively managed funds of DFA in every case. It did not matter whether the asset class was large caps or the supposedly inefficient classes of small caps and emerging markets.

The findings of all of the studies we have covered are exactly what the EMH predicts. Investors should not be able to outperform except as a result of random good luck. The studies all found that there is no persistence of outperformance beyond the randomly expected.

In addition to the evidence on the performance of pension plans, we also have evidence on the performance of 401(k) plans.

The Performance of Funds Offered by 401(k) Plans

The 401(k) plan was introduced in 1981. By year-end 2008, the total assets in these defined *contribution* plans had grown to over $2.3 trillion. The explosive growth has been fueled not only by the tax benefits they provide, but also by the demise of defined *benefit* plans—the kind that many corporations had historically provided. Given the amount of assets in these plans, as well as the fact that for over 60 percent of plan participants their 401(k) plan represents their sole financial asset outside of bank accounts, the actions of plan sponsors are vitally important.

Table 2.1   Comparative Returns, 1997–2009

Annualized Return (%)

Domestic Large Cap		Emerging Markets	
SEI Institutional Large Cap Growth A	3.1	SEI International Emerging Markets A	5.7
Russell US Core Equity I	4.3	Russell Emerging Markets S	7.7
DFA US Large Company	4.9	DFA Emerging Markets	9.2
Domestic Small Cap		**Developed International Market**	
SEI Institutional Small Cap Growth A	3.0	SEI International Trust Equity A	1.9
Russell US Small & Mid Cap I	6.4	Russell International Developed Markets I	4.0
DFA US Small Cap Portfolio	7.5	DFA Large Cap International	4.8
DFA US Micro Cap Portfolio	8.0	DFA International Value Portfolio III	7.4
Domestic Large Value		DFA International Small Company	6.7
SEI Institutional Large Cap Value A	5.1	DFA International Small Cap Value Portfolio Class I	8.3
DFA US Large Cap Value Class III	6.8		
Domestic Small Value			
SEI Institutional Small Cap Value A	8.0		
DFA US Small Cap Value	9.6		

Given the importance of these plans (and similar plans such as profit-sharing plans), investors should be aware of how well *plan sponsors* select mutual funds.

Professors Edwin J. Elton (NYU), Martin J. Gruber (NYU), and Christopher R. Blake (Fordham University) provided us with the answer to this and other questions in their 2006 study "Participant Reaction and the Performance of Funds Offered by 401(k) Plans."[4]

The authors examined the performance of all 401(k) plans that filed 11-K reports in 1994 and used publicly available mutual funds as choices offered to participants. They traced the sample through 1999. This database provided a sample of 289 plan years, representing 43 plans, most of which had seven years of data. Over these 289 plan years, 215 funds were added and 45 were dropped. The following is a review of their findings.

Fund Selection Skills

On average, plan sponsors select funds that outperform randomly selected funds of the same type. That provides an appearance of skill. However, because the alphas for the average plan were negative, performance would have improved if passive funds (such as index funds) had been substituted for the active funds actually chosen. The outperformance versus the random sample is likely the result of the fact that plans generally choose only funds from well-known fund families with a significant amount of assets under management. Mutual funds have economies of scale. Thus, funds with more assets can charge lower fees.

The authors also found that plan sponsors would have been best off imitating Rip Van Winkle.

Please Don't Do Something, Stand There

It seems that, just like individual investors, plan sponsors ignore the Securities and Exchange Commission (SEC) disclaimer about past performance not being a predictor of future performance. As one would expect, when plan sponsors change offerings, they choose funds that did well in the past. After all, who would choose a fund that had performed poorly? Funds that were added to plans had positive alphas for both one- and three-year periods prior to the change. And, unsurprisingly, managers fire poorly performing funds.

Funds that were dropped had negative alphas for both one- and three-year periods before they were dropped. Funds added had an alpha above those dropped of 2.8 percent per year for the three years before the change and 2.3 percent in the year before the change (note the declining alpha). Unfortunately, when a plan deleted a fund and replaced it with a fund with identical objectives, the deleted funds outperformed the ones they replaced by about 2.4 percent per annum over the next three years.

The authors also examined what happened when a plan replaced all of its offerings from one fund family and added funds from a new fund family. Not surprisingly, they found that the *past* Sharpe ratios (a measure of return relative to risk) were higher for the portfolio of added funds than for the portfolio of dropped funds. After replacement, the *future* Sharpe ratios were higher for the portfolio of dropped funds than for the funds they replaced. Once again, inaction would have proved better for investors than action.

Advice from Professional Investors

John R. Krimmel was the chief investment officer of the State Universities Retirement System of Illinois when he provided this insight on the likelihood of finding managers who will beat their benchmark. Commenting on the firings of the active fund managers the system had employed, he said:

> It's a tough area in which to operate. Academic research bears that out. Our experience shows that as well. Over the long haul we've just about broken even (that is, equaled the index return), but with slightly higher volatility.[5]

In 1997, Frederick Grauer was the cochairman of Barclays Global Investors—at the time the world's largest institutional fund manager. *Institutional Investor* magazine had declared 1997 to be "the year of the passive manager." The publication noted that managers known for their passive offerings not only racked up the largest gains as a group, but passive houses took both the gold and silver medals for gaining the most institutional assets. The magazine attributed the large gains made by the two firms to "the accelerating search by pension funds for consistent performance."

When asked about this trend, Grauer responded: "These trends, in conjunction with the growth of passive and enhanced indexers, have been major (market) drivers for the decade. In indexing people are looking to reduce costs and control exposures to the marketplace, to get exact implementation of pension policies. They are fed up with out-of-control outcomes."[6] And the trend has continued because of both the results produced by active managers and the publication of those results in academic papers.

Admissions from an Industry Practitioner

In 1996, Philip Halpern was the chief investment officer of the Washington State Investment Board (a large institutional investor). He and two of his coworkers wrote an article on their investment experiences. They wrote the article because their experience with active management was less than satisfactory and they knew, through their attendance at professional associations, that many of their colleagues shared, and therefore corroborated, their own experience. The article included a quote from a Goldman Sachs publication. As you read this, remember that Goldman is one of the largest active managers in the world: "Few managers consistently outperform the S&P 500. Thus, in the eyes of the plan sponsor, its plan is paying an excessive amount of the upside to the manager while still bearing substantial risk that its investments will achieve sub-par returns."

The article concluded, "Slowly, over time, many large pension funds have shared our experience and have moved toward indexing more domestic equity assets."[7]

We now turn to the evidence on hedge funds.

Chapter 3

Hedge Funds: The Evidence

We now have a significant body of research on the performance of hedge funds.

The 1999 study "Offshore Hedge Funds: Survival and Performance 1989–95" by Stephen J. Brown (professor of finance, NYU, Stern School of Business), William N. Goetzmann (professor of finance and management, International Center for Finance, Yale School of Management) and Roger G. Ibbotson (professor in the practice of finance at the Yale School of Management, and chairman and chief investment officer of Zebra Capital Management, LLC) found that most of the funds had underperformed the S&P 500 Index. Once again, there was no evidence of any persistent ability of managers in a particular style classification to earn returns in excess of their style benchmark.[1]

A *Forbes* article by columnist David Dreman presented a performance index of 2,600 hedge funds (1,500 domestic and 1,100 international) for the period from January 1993 to October 1998. After subtracting fees, the average annualized return of the hedge funds was 13.4 percent, trailing the 19.9 percent return of the S&P 500 by 6.5 percent.[2]

The 2006 study "The A, B, Cs of Hedge Funds: Alphas, Betas and Costs" by Roger G. Ibbotson and Peng Chen of Ibbotson Associates, covering the period from January 1995 through March 2006, found that the average hedge fund had returned 9.0 percent per year, lagging the S&P 500 by 2.6 percent per year. This study includes the bear market of 2000–2002 (the type of market when hedge funds are supposed to perform the best).[3]

The 2001 study "Hedge Fund Performance 1990–2000: Do the 'Money Machines' Really Add Value?" by Harry M. Kat (professor of risk management at the Cass Business School at City University, London) and Gaurav S. Amin investigated whether hedge funds did indeed offer investors a superior risk-adjusted return profile.[4] Because hedge fund returns may exhibit a high degree of non-normality (such as fat tails) as well as a nonlinear relationship with the stock market—rendering the use of traditional performance measures questionable—the study used a dynamic trading-based performance measure that does not require any assumptions about the distribution of fund returns.

The study covered 13 hedge fund indexes and 77 individual funds. The following is a summary of the authors' findings:

- Twelve of the 13 indexes (92 percent) showed signs of inefficiency, with the average efficiency loss (risk-adjusted return) on these 12 indexes amounting to 3.0 percent per year. In practical terms, this means that the same returns could have been achieved with much less risk.

- Of the 77 funds studied, 72 (94 percent) showed signs of inefficiency, with the average efficiency loss amounting to 7.0 percent per year. Only five funds offered superior performance, with an average efficiency gain of just 1.5 percent per year.
- All 15 of the event-driven funds showed signs of inefficiency, with an average efficiency loss of 3.8 percent per year.
- Of the 28 global hedge funds, 24 (86 percent) showed some level of inefficiency, with an average loss of 8.5 percent per year.
- Of the 11 market-neutral funds studied, 10 (91 percent) showed some level of inefficiency. For this group, the average efficiency loss was 6.8 percent per year.

The authors reached the conclusion that even without taking into account the significant survivorship bias that exists in hedge fund data, their results clearly contradict the claim that hedge funds generate superior investment results on a stand-alone basis.

The failure of hedge funds to deliver on their promise is readily apparent in the data in the Table 3.1.

The HFRX Index underperformed not only all the major equity asset classes, but they also underperformed fixed income indexes.

Just as was the case with mutual funds and pension plans, there is no evidence of any persistence of hedge fund performance beyond the randomly expected. Without persistence of performance, there is no way to identify the future alpha generators ahead of time.

Demonstrating this problem, Harry M. Kat's 2003 study "10 Things that Investors Should Know about Hedge Funds" found that for the period from 1994 to 2001, the average fund of hedge funds underperformed an equally weighted portfolio

Table 3.1 Investment Returns, 2003–2009

	Annualized Return (%)
HFRX Index	2.4
Domestic Indexes	
S&P 500	5.5
MSCI US Small Cap 1750	9.9
MSCI US Prime Market Value	6.0
MSCI US Small Cap Value	9.3
Dow Jones Select REIT	8.8
International Indexes	
MSCI EAFE	10.3
MSCI EAFE Small Cap	14.5
MSCI EAFE Value	11.4
MSCI Emerging Markets	22.0
Fixed Income	
Merrill Lynch One-Year Treasury Note	2.9
Five-Year Treasury Notes	4.2
Twenty-Year Treasury Bonds	5.1

Source: MSCI Inc., S&P, and Barclays

of randomly selected (from the sample) hedge funds by 3 percent per year.[5]

And there are many more problems with hedge funds.

The Problems with Hedge Funds

1. *Lack of liquidity.* Unlike mutual fund investors, hedge fund investors typically must accept long lock-up periods. In addition, redemption rights (the ability to withdraw assets from the fund) can be suspended. Liquidity is a risk for

which investors should receive additional compensation. The evidence shows that there has not been any compensation for this incremental risk.

2. *Transparency.* Because hedge funds lack transparency, investors lose control over their asset allocation, the most important determinant of the risk of a portfolio.

3. *Non-normal distribution of returns.* Hedge funds exhibit characteristics that risk-averse investors dislike, and the majority of investors are risk averse. Hedge funds exhibit both negative skewness (the opposite of a lottery ticket, where most people lose, but losses are small and a few winners win big) and high kurtosis. Assets that exhibit high kurtosis produce exceptional returns (both high and low) with greater-than-normal frequency—so-called fat tails.

4. *Risk of "dying."* The risk of a hedge fund dying (shutting down) is so great that the 2005 study "Hedge Funds: Risk and Return" by Burton G. Malkiel and Atanu Saha found that survivorship bias in the reported data on hedge fund returns creates an incredibly large upward bias of 4.4 percent per year. The same study found that there is a substantial attrition rate—less than 25 percent of the funds in existence in 1996 were still alive in 2004. The difference in returns between the live and defunct funds exceeded 8 percent per year (13.7 versus 5.4).[6]

   The 2002 study "Hedge Fund Survival Lifetimes" by Greg N. Gregoriou (professor of finance in the School of Business and Economics, State University of New York, Plattsburgh) covered the period from 1990 to 2001 and found that the median residual lifetime of a fund is just 5.5 years.[7]

5. *Riskiness of the assets.* A study by hedge fund AQR Capital Management, covering the six-year period ending January 31, 2001, found that many hedge funds were taking on significantly greater risk by investing in illiquid securities.[8]

And many hedge funds use leverage to try and enhance returns. Thus, the alphas reported by hedge funds are misleading, as they use inappropriate (less risky) benchmarks. The study "The Performance of Hedge Funds: Risk, Return and Incentives" concluded: "Hedge funds provided greater returns than mutual funds, but provided no advantage over indexing on a risk-adjusted basis."[9]

6. *Tax inefficiencies.* Due to high turnover rates, the average hedge fund produces returns in a tax-inefficient manner.

7. *Agency risk.* The compensation structure of hedge funds is geared so that most of the reward managers receive occurs in the form of incentive pay (usually 20 percent of profits). Investors take all the downside risk, but do not participate fully in the upside. Agency risk occurs when a manager approaches the end of a year and has failed to reach the benchmark level above which incentive compensation is paid. This presents a clear conflict of interest in the form of unequal incentives. If the manager takes large risks in an attempt to beat the benchmark and wins, he will receive incentive pay. However, if the manager fails, he loses nothing and still receives the minimum fee. This creates an incentive for the fund manager to take on greater risk in a game of "I Can Win but I Never Lose." Note that agency risk is reduced if the manager invests significant amounts of his or her own assets in the fund.

What has happened in the past, leading to the eventual demise of several hedge funds, is that a trader places a bet that loses. He decides to double up in an effort to earn back the loss. If the market keeps going against the trader, he doubles up again until the "game" ends.

There is a second type of agency risk. Most hedge funds have a clause that "protects" investors with what is known as a "high-water mark," which works in the following manner. After a year of negative performance, the fund cannot collect its incentive pay unless it first "makes up" the negative performance.

For example, if a fund loses 10 percent in the first year, its incentive pay in the second year will be calculated only on the amount earned above the high-water mark. Due to the effect of compounding, the fund would have to earn 11.1 percent in the second year to return to the high-water mark.

The problem for investors is twofold. First, the same type of agency risk just discussed becomes an issue. To reach the high-water mark and earn the incentive compensation, the fund manager may be tempted to take on greater risk than anticipated by investors.

The second problem is that after a bad year or two, when the chances of earning any incentive pay become small, the fund manager has the right to shut down the fund, returning all assets to investors—the high-water mark that investors counted on never comes into play. The hedge fund manager leaves and starts up a new fund with no high-water mark to overcome.

Agency risk can also appear in the form of outright fraud.

8. *Biases in the data.* When investors look at the performance of hedge funds, they need to be aware that the data is likely to be misleading—the returns are overstated by biases in the data. The biases in the data include the previously mentioned survivorship bias (4.4 percent per year) and instant history (also known as backfill) bias. The aforementioned study "Hedge Funds: Risk and Return" found that the backfill bias was over 5 percent per year.[10] There is yet another bias known as self-selection bias. (Poorly performing funds choose not to report.) Unfortunately, we cannot know how much of a bias that adds to the data.

And we are not yet done. There is one more important and large bias in the data—liquidation bias. This phenomenon occurs in the data because funds that become defunct often fail to report their last returns. While it is impossible to know for certain the full impact of liquidation bias, "A Reality Check on Hedge Funds," a 2003 paper by Nolke Posthuma (ABP Investments, Netherlands) and Pieter Jelle van der Sluis (assistant professor, Free University of Amsterdam), estimated the effect based on conversations with employees of Tass, the repository of the largest database on hedge funds (now owned by Lipper).

The assumption is that the hedge funds that terminated their reporting did so due to serious negative performance. The most famous example is Long-Term Capital Management, which managed to lose 92 percent of its capital from October 1997 through October 1998 and did not report that loss to public databases.

The authors of the paper added one final month to returns to estimate the impact of liquidation bias. They created two scenarios—one with an estimate of a 50 percent loss and the other with an estimated loss of 100 percent. An assumption of a 50 percent loss created a liquidation bias of about 3 percent. A 100 percent loss assumption created a liquidation bias of 6 percent.[11]

If we add all the biases together, the total would approach, or perhaps exceed, 10 percent.

Advice from Professional Investors and Academics

David Swensen, chief investment officer of the Yale Endowment Fund, made the following observation:

In the hedge fund world, as in the whole of the money management industry, consistent, superior active management constitutes a rare commodity. Assuming that active managers of hedge funds achieve success levels similar to active managers of traditional marketable securities, investors in hedge funds face dramatically higher levels of prospective failure due to the materially higher levels of fees.[12]

Swensen had this to say on funds of hedge funds:

> Fund of funds are a cancer on the institutional-investor world. They facilitate the flow of ignorant capital.[13]

Professor Eugene F. Fama is the Robert R. McCormick Distinguished Service Professor of Finance at the University of Chicago Booth School of Business. He is often thought of as the father of the Efficient Market Hypothesis (EMH). Fama offered the following advice for those considering investing in hedge funds:

> If you want to invest in something (hedge funds) where they steal your money and don't tell you what they're doing, be my guest.[14]

Laurence Kotlikoff is a professor of economics at Boston University and was a senior economist for the President's Council of Economic Advisors. Scott Burns has been a personal financial columnist for over 40 years. The two are co-authors of *Spend 'til the End*. They noted:

> Prostitution may be the world's oldest profession, but selling risky investments is surely the most lucrative.[15]

Gary Weiss is an investigative journalist, columnist, and author of two books that critically examine the ethics and morality of Wall Street. In his book, *Wall Street versus America*, Weiss warned investors:

> Hedge funds are the only component of Wall Street that is built pretty much entirely upon myth. Few areas of financial endeavor

have been a subject of so many hoary myths, moronic half-truths, goofy speculation, once-true falsehoods, and knucklehead fantasies.[16]

Weiss added this warning:

Usually the financial press . . . forgets to mention that the superstar investors tended to make their biggest bucks when they were managing small sums of money. Some of the biggest names in the business liquidated or wound down their funds when their assets swelled beyond reasonable size, the odds caught up with them, and their performance turned lousy.[17]

If you are interested in learning more about hedge funds, my book (co-authored with Jared Kizer), *The Only Guide to Alternative Investments You'll Ever Need,* has a chapter dedicated to the subject.

Chapter 4

Private Equity/ Venture Capital: The Evidence

A s is the case with mutual funds and hedge funds, we have a substantial body of academic research on private equity/venture capital. As you will see, the studies all come to the same conclusion—private equity has not outperformed publicly available mutual funds on a risk-adjusted basis. And that does not even account for the liquidity that private equity investors forfeit. Let's examine the evidence.

According to Venture Economics (a research firm that provides information and analysis on the private equity industry), private equity overall returned 13.8 percent for the 20-year period ending June 30, 2005, outperforming the S&P 500 Index by 2.6 percent per annum.[1] However, venture capital investments are certainly more risky than investing in the

S&P 500. Therefore, we need to consider how other equity asset classes of more similar risk performed. While private equity capital outperformed the S&P 500, it underperformed more similarly risky small-cap value stocks that returned 16.0 percent.

The data from Venture Economics also allows us to examine the returns of three subsectors of the private equity market: venture capital, leveraged buyouts (LBOs), and mezzanine financing. LBOs involve acquiring businesses using mostly debt and a small amount of equity, with the debt being secured by the assets of the business. Mezzanine financings are late-stage venture capital investments, usually the final round of financing prior to an initial public offering (IPO). As later stage investments, mezzanine financings are less risky. Thus, capital provided in mezzanine financings is typically less costly than earlier stage investments. On the whole, venture capital (the riskiest of private equity investments) just matched the 16 percent return of small-cap value stocks. And, as we would expect, because of its greater risk, early-stage venture capital (i.e., seed capital) provided the highest return—20.2 percent. Later-stage venture capital, despite the still significant risks, actually underperformed the returns of small-cap value public equities, returning 13.8 percent. LBOs also returned 13.8 percent, and mezzanine financing returned just 9.1 percent.[2]

These findings are consistent with those of the study "Private Equity Performance: Returns, Persistence and Capital Flows," by authors Steve Kaplan (professor of entrepreneurship and finance, University of Chicago, Booth School of Business) and Antoinette Schoar (professor of entrepreneurial finance, MIT, Sloan School of Management). The study covered private equity funds that launched from 1980 to 1997, although the data covered the period ending in 2001. The authors found that the average private equity fund had, net of fees, returns roughly equal to the return of the S&P 500.[3]

The aforementioned research covered the period that included one of the greatest private equity booms in history—the Internet/dot-com era. It is helpful to also examine returns from an earlier period. The 1992 study "Venture Capital at the Crossroads" by William D. Bygrave (professor emeritus, Babson) and Jeffry A. Timmons (professor of entrepreneurship, Babson), covering the period from 1974 to 1989, found that the average internal rate of return (IRR) from venture capital was 13.5 percent.[4] (The IRR is the discount or interest rate at which the net present value of an investment is equal to zero.) This was virtually identical to the 13.3 percent return from the S&P 500. However, this was significantly below the returns of micro-cap stocks (17.5 percent) and small-cap value stocks (23.7 percent).

We also have the results of a 2002 study on private equity premiums by Tobias J. Moskowitz (professor of finance, University of Chicago, Booth School of Business) and Annette Vissing-Jorgensen (associate professor of finance, Northwestern, Kellogg School of Management), covering the period from 1952 through 1999. The authors concluded that private equity investing provided returns similar to those of public equity markets. They noted that the finding was surprising, given the greater risks of private equity investing. For example, they found that after 10 years the survival rate of private firms was only about 34 percent—there is a high risk of a total loss.[5]

The results of the 2007 study "The Performance of Private Equity Funds" by Oliver Gottschalg (assistant professor of strategy, HEC Business School, Paris) and Ludovic Phalippou (associate professor of finance, University of Amsterdam) are quite interesting. The authors researched the performance of 6,000 private equity deals and about 1,000 buyout funds, using data collected from investors in 852 private equity funds raised before 1993 (to be sure the funds had sold all their assets). They found that *after* accounting for fees, the average private equity fund *underperformed* the S&P 500 by 3 percent per year.[6]

Finally, we have the 2005 study "The Risk and Returns of Venture Capital" by John H. Cochrane (professor of finance, University of Chicago, Booth School of Business), which covered the period from 1987 through June 2000. Cochrane looked at 16,613 financing rounds involving 7,765 companies and found the returns to venture capital were similar to those of the smallest Nasdaq stocks. These are stocks defined by small market capitalizations that are illiquid and thinly traded. (For some of them, there are many months with no trading at all.) Furthermore, they exhibit traits similar to venture capital (extreme skewness and high volatility). Despite their greater risks, venture capital did not provide any higher return than comparable publicly traded equities. Cochrane concluded: "The fact that we see a similar phenomenon in public and private markets suggests that there is little that is special about venture capital."[7]

Summarizing the results of the research, private equity strategies have provided returns that have not been commensurate with the risks involved. Among the considerations are that private equity investors forgo the benefits of liquidity, transparency, broad diversification, and access to daily pricing that mutual fund investors enjoy. Also keep in mind that private equity investments typically entail long lockout periods, during which investors cannot access their capital. In addition, there are other aspects of the asset class that investors should consider carefully.

Characteristics of Private Equity Returns

Studies have found that private equity returns exhibit the following characteristics:

- *Extreme positive skewness in returns.* The median return of private equity is much lower than the mean (the arithmetic average) return. Their relatively high average return reflects the small possibility of a truly outstanding return, combined with the much larger probability of a more modest or negative return. In effect, private equity investments are like options (or lottery tickets): They provide a small chance of a huge payout, but a much larger chance of a below-average return. This is what is meant by positive skewness.[8]

- *High standard deviation of returns.* The standard deviation of private equity is in excess of 100 percent. This compares to the standard deviations of the S&P 500 of about 20 percent, and of small-cap value stocks (the Fama/French small-cap value index) of about 35 percent from 1927 to 2007. The 2002 study "Venture Capital and Its Role in Strategic Asset Allocation" covered the period from 1960 through 1999 and found that venture capital had an annual arithmetic average return of 45 percent. The high standard deviation of 116 percent reduced the annual arithmetic average return of 45 percent to an *annualized* return of just 13 percent. Authors Peng Chen (president and chief investment officer, Ibbotson Associates), Gary T. Baierl (head of quantitative research, Causeway Capital Management) and Paul D. Kaplan (director of research, Morningstar) concluded: "The variance of VC investment is so high that the estimated average compounded annual return for VC investment is actually lower than for U.S. small-cap stocks and comparable to U.S. large-cap stocks and international stocks."[9]

In addition to the risks of extreme skewness and high volatility, investors must consider that because of the inability to broadly diversify across hundreds or even thousands of stocks (as do index/passive asset class mutual funds), private equity investing involves accepting the risk that such investments may produce a wide dispersion of returns. Because of the size of their portfolios, institutional investors are able to diversify their exposure to private equity investments across many investments. It is unlikely that the typical individual investor would be able to accomplish similar diversification. Thus, it is unlikely that the returns individual investors received over the period would have been similar to the 13.8 percent return averaged by all private equity funds. Without such diversification, investors must accept the risk that the funds they invest in might generate poor results. Therefore, one of the risks individual investors are accepting, probably without giving it appropriate consideration, is an *uncompensated* risk—because it could be diversified away.

Bias in the Data

Despite the less-than-favorable results, the data actually contains an upward bias. The aforementioned study "The Performance of Private Equity Funds" attempted to correct for this bias.[10] The bias results from what the authors called "living dead" investments. In other words, the residual values reported in studies often includes inactive funds—those with an age above the typical age limit of funds (i.e., 10 years) that show no sign of any recent activity within the past four years, such as distributions or cash calls. As a result, accounting values may not reflect market values. Poorly performing funds have an incentive to postpone liquidation to artificially raise their reported return. Thus, the authors suggest that the residual value of these funds is overstated (and should likely be written off).

Studies that include only liquidated funds (such as the one by Kaplan and Schoar) have a "winner's" bias. Once the authors of the paper corrected for this bias, they found the return of private equity funds raised between 1980 and 1996 lagged the return of the S&P 500 by 3.3 percent per annum. They also found that about one-quarter of the funds had negative

IRRs and that few funds produced very high returns—the distribution of returns has similarities to a lottery ticket.

Advice from a Professional Investor

In his book *Pioneering Portfolio Management*, Yale's chief investment officer, David Swensen, described his unconventional approach to institutional investing. Swensen recommended that institutional investors capture the liquidity premium available in illiquid investments. Endowments differ from individual investors because of their very long investment horizons, allowing them to take liquidity risk that would be inappropriate for individual investors. Thus, the "Yale model" is characterized by relatively heavy exposure to asset classes such as private equity.

After the success of his first book, Swensen went on to write *Unconventional Success*. He planned to show individual investors how to invest the "Yale way." When it came to the actual writing, Swensen realized that the "Yale model" was not appropriate for individuals because they are different in many ways from institutional investors:

> Understanding the difficulty of identifying superior hedge-fund, venture-capital, and leveraged-buyout investments leads to the conclusion that hurdles for casual investors stand insurmountably high. Even many well-equipped investors fail to clear the hurdles necessary to achieve consistent success in producing market-beating active management results. When operating in arenas that depend fundamentally on active management for success, ill-informed manager selection poses grave risks to portfolio assets.[11]

If you are interested in learning more about venture capital, my book *The Only Guide to Alternative Investments You'll Ever Need* has a chapter dedicated to the subject.

We now turn to the evidence on individual investors.

Chapter 5

Individual Investors: The Evidence

B rad M. Barber (professor of finance, UC Davis, Graduate School of Management) and Terrance Odean (professor of banking and finance, University of California, Berkeley, Haas School of Business) have done a series of groundbreaking studies on investor behavior and its impact on investment returns. Their body of work provides us with a wealth of evidence on individual investors.

Their study "Boys Will Be Boys: Gender, Overconfidence, and Common Stock Investment" examined the role that gender played in investment returns.[1] The study covered the performance of 35,000 households at a large brokerage house from February 1991 to January 1997. The following is a summary of their findings:

- Men traded 45 percent more than women.
- Turnover reduced net returns by 2.65 percent per annum for men versus 1.72 per annum for women.

- The turnover of single men was 67 percent greater than that of single women, presumably because of the lack of influence from their more cautious spouses. The increased turnover cost men 1.44 percent per annum.
- Both men and women underperformed market and risk-adjusted benchmarks.
- The stocks that both men and women bought trailed the market *after* they bought them, and the stocks they sold outperformed *after* they were sold. Both sexes would have been better off if they had simply held the portfolios they began with.
- Those that traded the most performed the worst.

In Odean's study "Do Investors Trade Too Much?," he found that the average return to purchased securities was 3.3 percent less than the average return of sold securities over the next year. In his conclusion, Odean noted, "Even when trading costs are ignored, these investors actually lower their returns through trading."[2]

The results of these studies are consistent with those of the 1977 study "Patterns of Investment Strategy and Behavior among Individual Investors."[3] This study covered the trading patterns of 972 individuals. The following are its main conclusions:

- Men spent more time and dollars on investment research.
- Men relied less on advisers/brokers.
- Men made more trades than women, producing higher turnover.
- Men believed returns were more predictable.

The authors believe that all of the above are evidence that men are overconfident of their skills relative to women. They also hypothesized that men may have a greater preference for gambling than women, accounting for their greater trading activity and lower net returns.

The results of the two studies provide evidence that neither men nor women seem to have learned much about their investment skills (or lack of them) since 1977—they don't learn from their experiences, a behavior Einstein defined as insanity.

Barber and Odean also studied the performance of investment clubs—perhaps more heads are better than one. Their study "Too Many Cooks Spoil the Profit: Investment Club Performance" covered 166 investment clubs using data from a large brokerage house from February 1991 to January 1997.[4] Here is a summary of their findings:

- The average club lagged a broad market index by 3.8 percent per annum, returning 14.1 percent versus 17.9 percent.
- When performance was adjusted for exposure to the risk factors of size and value, alphas were negative even before transactions costs. After trading costs (turnover averaged 65 percent) the alphas were on average −4.4 percent per annum.
- The clubs would have been far better off if they had never traded during the year—beginning-of-the-year portfolios outperformed their actual holdings by 3.5 percent per annum. The reason was that the stocks they sold outperformed the stocks they bought by over 4 percent per annum. The conclusion is that investment clubs have something in common with individual investors—trading is hazardous to their financial health.

Examining the results of the Mensa investment club provides an amusing bit of evidence on the ability of individual investors to produce alpha. It seems logical that if any group of individuals could beat the market, it would be the members of the Mensa club. Mensa is the largest and best-known society of people with high IQs—98th percentile or higher. The June 2001 issue of *Smart Money* reported that over the prior 15 years, the Mensa investment club returned just 2.5 percent, underperforming the S&P 500 Index by almost 13 percent per annum. Warren Smith, an investor for 35 years, reported that his original investment of $5,300 had turned into $9,300. A similar investment in the S&P 500 would have produced almost $300,000. One investor described their strategy as buy low, sell lower.

Investment Returns versus Investor Returns

The returns reported by mutual funds are called time-weighed returns (TWRs). TWRs eliminate the effect of additions and withdrawals to the portfolio. The effect of varying cash inflows is eliminated by assuming a single investment at the beginning of a period and measuring the growth or loss of market value to the end of that period. Investors, however, earn dollar-weighted returns (DWRs) that are impacted by the timing of additions and withdrawals. Therefore, the DWR can differ greatly from the reported TWR.

Morningstar studied the performance of mutual funds and their investors. They found that in all 17 fund categories they examined, the returns earned by investors were below the returns of the funds themselves. For example, among large-cap growth funds, the 10-year annualized DWR was 3.4 percent less than the TWR. For mid- and small-cap growth funds, the underperformance was 2.5 and 3.0 percent. Investors in sector funds fared worse, with tech investors producing particularly disastrous results, underperforming the very funds they invested in by 14 percent per annum. Health care investors underperformed by 4 percent per annum, and investors in financial sector funds underperformed by 1.6 percent per annum. Even value investors fared poorly, though their underperformance was not as severe. Large-cap value investors underperformed the funds they invest in by 0.4 percent per annum, and small-cap value investors underperformed by 2.0 percent per annum.[5]

Morningstar has also found that volatile funds (often focused on one sector) tend to have the greatest discrepancies between TWR and DWR. They note: "Volatile funds may entice investors on the upswing, but spook them into withdrawing during rough patches. So, investors in volatile funds can unwittingly end up buying high and selling low." They provided examples demonstrating how destructive investor behavior can be. The returns are for the five-year period ending July 2009:

Fund	TWR (Investment Return) (%)	DWR (Investor Return) (%)	Gap (%)
CGM Focus (CGMFX)	8.8	−18.3	27.1
Fairholme (FAIRX)	8.6	−1.7	10.3
Schneider Value (SCMLX)	−4.0	−18.8	14.4

As bad as those figures are, the damage was even worse for the one fund for which 10-year data was available, CGM Focus. The TWR was 17.8 percent, while the DWR was −16.8, producing a gap of an incredible 34.6 percent per annum.[6]

We also have evidence from a study done by the Bogle Financial Markets Center. The sample consisted of the 200 funds with the largest cash inflows for the five-year period 1996 through 2000. The study compared the TWR of the funds and the DWR of investors in those funds for the 10-year period 1996−2005. The average TWR for the 200 mutual funds was 8.9 percent per annum. However, the actual DWR earned by investors was just 2.4 percent annum, an investment gap of 6.5 percent per annum. Investor behavior resulted in the DWR's being just 27 percent of the TWR. The study also found that the TWR exceeded the DWR in all but two

Table 5.1   Fund Return versus Shareholder Return, 1998–2001

Fund	Fund Return (%)	Shareholder Return (%)	Cost of Investor Behavior (%)
Fidelity Aggressive Growth	2.8	−24.1	−26.9
Vanguard Capital Opportunity	29.2	5.2	−23.9
Invesco Dynamics	7.0	−14.4	−21.4
Janus Mercury	13.9	−7.4	−21.3
Fidelity Select Electronics	21.7	7.6	−14.0

of the 200 funds—and there was not a single case where the DWR exceeded the TWR by more than 0.5 percent. Even more shocking was that in the case of 76 funds, the cumulative shortfall ranged from −50 percent to −95 percent.[7]

Finally, consider this tale of woe. For the four-year period 1998–2001, the annualized return of the average mutual fund was 5.7 percent. Unfortunately, the average investor earned just 1 percent—a loss of 82 percent of the available returns. *Investor behavior* created an *investment gap* of 4.7 percent. Table 5.1 shows the five largest gaps between fund returns and investor returns. It shows how costly investor behavior can be.[8]

Advice from Professional Investors and Academics

David Swensen offered this advice:

> Sophisticated institutional investors dominate the marketable security landscape, aggressively competing to unearth the rare security that promises risk-adjusted excess returns. Individuals who attempt

to compete with resource-rich money management organizations simply provide fodder for large institutional cannon.[9]

Terrance Odean offered the following advice on investing in individual stocks.

> The point seems to be that individual investors for the most part shouldn't be trying to pick stocks. They did worse than if they had been throwing darts.[10]

As to investment clubs, Odean offered this advice:

> Investment clubs serve many useful functions. They encourage savings. They educate their members about financial markets. They foster friendships and social ties. They entertain. Unfortunately, their investments do not beat the market.[11]

Thomas Gilovich is a professor and chairman of the psychology department at Cornell University. He is also the co-author (along with Gary Belsky) of *Why Smart People Make Big Money Mistakes,* as well as many articles on behavioral finance. He states:

> Any individual who is not professionally occupied in the financial services industry (and even most of those who are) and who in any way attempts to actively manage an investment portfolio is probably suffering from overconfidence. That is, anyone who has confidence enough in his or her abilities and knowledge to invest in a particular stock or bond (or actively managed mutual fund or real estate investment trust or limited partnership) is most likely fooling himself. In fact, most such people—probably you—have no business at all trying to pick investments, except perhaps as sport. Such people—again, probably you—should simply divide their money among several index mutual funds and turn off CNBC.[12]

Daniel Kahneman is a professor of psychology and public affairs at Princeton University and a Nobel Laureate. He is considered one of the founding fathers of the field of behavioral finance.

What's really quite remarkable in the investment world is that people are playing a game which, in some sense, cannot be played. There are so many people out there in the market; the idea that any single individual without extra information or extra market power can beat the market is extraordinarily unlikely. Yet the market is full of people who think they can do it and full of other people who believe them. This is one of the great mysteries of finance: Why do people believe they can do the impossible? And why do other people believe them?

Kahneman continued:

People see skill in performance where there is no skill.[13]

Richard Thaler is a professor of behavioral science and economics at the Booth School of Business at the University of Chicago. He is best known for his collaborations with Kahneman. A *New York Times* article stated:

Professor Thaler and Robert J. Shiller, an economics professor at Yale, note that individual investors and money managers persist in their beliefs that they are endowed with more and better information than others, and that they can profit by picking stocks. Sobering experience can help those who delude themselves. But not always. That people "do not learn to correct most of their tendencies to overconfidence is apparently just one of the limitations of the human mind," Professor Shiller wrote in an article available on the World Wide Web.[14]

Merton Miller shared the Nobel Prize in economics in 1990 with Harry Markowitz and William Sharpe. He was on the faculty of the University of Chicago Graduate School of Business from 1961 until his retirement in 1993. He also served as a director on the Chicago Board of Trade and the Chicago Mercantile Exchange from 1990 until his death in June 2000. Miller warned investors:

I make my money writing about the market, not participating in it.[15]

Admissions from Industry Practitioners and the Financial Media

Holman Jenkins Jr., a member of the editorial board of the *Wall Street Journal*, writes:

> Why is there a whole industry devoted to helping individual investors pick out stocks when every jot of financial wisdom in the past 50 years, including Nobel prize–winning work, suggests that this is a mug's game?[16]

Wall Street Journal columnist Jonathan Clements made the following observation: "Beat the market? The idea is ludicrous. Very few investors manage to beat the market. But in an astonishing triumph of hope over experience, millions of investors keep trying."[17]

Henry Blodget was the former senior Internet analyst for CIBC Oppenheimer who was later employed by Merrill Lynch. In 2003, the Securities and Exchange Commission (SEC) charged him with securities fraud. He settled without admitting or denying the allegations and was subsequently barred from the securities industry for life. He paid a $2 million fine and $2 million disgorgement. Writing for Slate.com, Blodgett recommends:

> The way to give yourself the best chance of success in the markets is to diversify, buy low-cost funds, and hold them forever. That's it.[18]

Robert Barker is a senior writer for *BusinessWeek*, covering investments and personal finance. He writes the weekly column "The Barker Portfolio." He had also worked at *Barron's* and *SmartMoney*. Given the nature of his column, you might be surprised at the advice he offered:

> Yet even the smartest, most determined fund picker can't escape a host of nasty surprises.

He also noted:

Next time you're tempted to buy anything other than an index fund, remember this—and think again.[19]

We now turn to the evidence from the field of behavioral finance.

Chapter 6

Behavioral Finance: The Evidence

Behavioral finance is the study of human behavior and how that behavior leads to investment errors, including the mispricing of assets. The field has gained an increasing amount of attention in academia over the past 15 years or so as pricing anomalies have been discovered. Pricing anomalies present a problem for those who believe in the Efficient Market Hypothesis (EMH). However, the real question for investors is not whether the market persistently makes pricing errors. Instead, the real question is: are the anomalies exploitable after taking into account real-world costs? In other words, if behavioral finance is to have merit as an alternative investment strategy to passive investing, one should be able to observe investors who have successfully utilized its theories and produced abnormal returns.

The authors of the study "Behavioral Finance: Are the Disciples Profiting from the Doctrine?" identified 16 self-proclaimed or media-identified behavioral mutual funds—funds that attempt to take advantage of discoveries from the field of behavioral finance.[1] For example, the managers of one fund offer the following on their Web site:

> Investors make mental mistakes that can cause stocks to be mispriced. Fuller & Thaler's objective is to use our understanding of human decision making to find these mispriced stocks and earn superior returns.[2]

The authors analyzed the behavioral funds to determine whether they successfully attract investment dollars and also if their strategies earn abnormal returns for their investors. The following summarizes their findings:

- Behavioral funds successfully attracted investment dollars at a significantly greater rate than index and corresponding actively managed nonbehavioral funds. Investors apparently believe that the pricing errors are persistently exploitable.
- While the funds do outperform S&P 500 Index funds, the explanation for the outperformance is that they load very heavily on the HML (high minus low) factor (meaning they have significant exposure to value stocks). After adjusting for risk, they do not earn abnormal returns.
- Behavioral mutual funds are tantamount to value investing and not much more.

There Is Smoke, but No Fire

While behavioral finance has gained substantial attention in academia and seems to be gaining greater acceptance among practitioners, there doesn't seem to be any evidence to support the raison d'etre for the funds—anomalies can be identified and exploited on a persistent basis. Even if there are anomalies, there are two simple and plausible explanations for the findings of the study. The first is that strategies have no costs, but implementing them does. A strategy may appear to work on paper, but the costs of implementation can exceed the size of the pricing errors. The second is that once an anomaly is discovered, and attempts are made to exploit it, the very act of doing it will serve to eliminate/reduce the size of the pricing error.

Those who seek to exploit market anomalies almost inevitably find that the markets are tyrannical in their efficiency. The following examples will demonstrate that point.

The Tyranny of the Efficient Markets

Richard Thaler, professor of behavioral science and economics at the Booth School of Business at the University of Chicago, is one of the leaders in the field of behavioral finance. As we discussed, the basic hypothesis of behavioral finance is that, due to behavioral biases, markets make persistent mistakes in pricing securities. An example of a persistent mistake is that the market underreacts to news—both good and bad news are only slowly incorporated into prices. Fuller and Thaler Asset Management was formed to exploit such errors.

Fuller and Thaler offer two funds based on behavioral theories: Undiscovered Managers Behavioral Growth Fund and Undiscovered Managers Behavioral Value Fund. (Note that JPMorgan acquired these funds in January 2004. However, Fuller continues as a subadviser.) To test their theories, we will compare the performance of these funds to the performance of the Dimensional Fund Advisors (DFA) Small Cap Fund and its Small Value Fund, respectively. The DFA funds are managed based on the belief that markets are efficient, so stock selection and market-timing efforts are eschewed. Thus, we have a real live test of the behavioral theory and the efficiency of the market.

For the 10-year period 2000–2009, the Behavioral Growth Fund returned −2.0 percent per year. This compares to the 5.7 percent per year return of the DFA Small Cap Fund. The Behavioral Growth Fund even underperformed the S&P 500 by 1 percent per year. The Behavioral Value Fund returned 7.8 percent per annum. The DFA Small Value Fund returned 9.1 percent. The two Behavioral Funds provided an average return of 2.9 percent, compared to the 7.4 percent average return of the two DFA funds. There certainly doesn't seem to be any evidence of the ability to exploit inefficiencies in the market.

Further Evidence

LSV Asset Management (LSV) was formed in 1994 by professors Josef Lakonishok (University of Illinois at Urbana-Champaign), Andrei Shleifer (Harvard University), and Robert Vishny (formerly of the University of Chicago). Together, they have published over 200 academic papers on investing and the field of behavioral finance. Their research is the foundation for LSV's investment strategy. The basic premise of their investment strategy is that superior long-term results can be achieved by systematically exploiting the judgmental biases and behavioral weaknesses that influence the decisions of many investors. These include the tendency to: (1) extrapolate the past too far into the future, (2) wrongly equate a good company with a good investment irrespective of price, (3) ignore statistical evidence and (4) develop a "mind-set" about a company. They believe that the market persistently misprices securities and that pricing mistakes can be exploited.

While LSV is basically an institutional money manager, it runs three mutual funds: the LSV Value Equity Fund (LSVEX), the LSV Conservative Value Equity Fund (LSVVX), and the LSV Conservative Core Equity Fund (LSVPX). Lakonishok, the chief executive officer of LSV, also manages the HighMark Small Cap Value Fund (HMSCX).

To test whether the hypothesized inefficiencies can be exploited, we can compare the performance of these funds against the passively managed funds of DFA. Since both LSVVX and LSVPX have inception dates of 2007, and we want to look at longer-term data, we will confine our comparison to just the other two funds.

Again, we look at the 10-year period 2000–2009. LSVEX returned 5.0 percent per year. The similar DFA Large Cap Value Fund returned 4.4 percent per annum. Thus, the LSV fund outperformed a passive benchmark by 0.6 percent per annum. So far, so good. Now let's look at the performance of HMSCX. It returned 7.7 percent per year. The similar DFA Small Cap Value Fund returned 9.1 percent per annum—the behavioral fund underperformed a passive benchmark by 1.4 percent per annum.

The average annualized return of the two behavioral funds that were trying to exploit market inefficiencies was 6.4 percent per annum. The two similar passively managed funds provided an average annualized return of 6.8 percent per annum. Based on this evidence, it seems that exploiting inefficiencies is a lot harder than identifying them.

The Failed Quest

We have seen how the some of the leading academics have applied their theories on market inefficiency and failed in their quest for the Holy Grail of alpha. There does not seem to be evidence in favor of the behavioral theory being an implementable strategy. The case can be made that if there ever was a time when the theory would have worked, it no longer appears to be true. The tyranny of the efficiency of markets and the wisdom of crowds is a very powerful opponent indeed.

The Value of Behavioral Finance

Despite its inability to provide us with an investment strategy that can be used to deliver alpha, the field of behavioral finance does provide us with guidance to help avoid investment mistakes. As the January 1997 edition of *Institutional Investor* observed:

- "People often see order where it doesn't exist and interpret accidental success to be the result of skill."
- "Most investors see other people's decisions as the results of their disposition but their own choices as rational."
- "People often treat the highly probable as certain and the improbable as impossible."
- "Investors typically give too much weight to a recent experience. Recent gains beget overconfidence; recent losses, overcautiousness."

Even Smart People Make Mistakes

While even smart people make mistakes, once they learn that the behavior was a mistake, they don't repeat it—that is the behavior of fools. The necessary condition for investors to learn is that they must actually know what happened in the past and that their views of the past are not biased. Unfortunately, the evidence suggests that, in general, investors do not learn from experience—and, therefore, they keep making the same mistakes. Why is this? One explanation is that they don't even know they are making mistakes. The study "Why Inexperienced Investors Do Not Learn: They Don't Know Their Past Portfolio Performance" found evidence supporting this explanation.[3]

Authors Markus Glaser and Martin Weber analyzed the actual performance of the online brokerage accounts of individual investors. One objective was to determine how well investors knew what returns they actually earned. Thus, they compared the actual results to the answers the investors provided on a questionnaire. The following is a summary of their findings:

- Investors are unable to give a correct estimate of their own past portfolio performance.
- On average, investors underperformed relevant benchmarks. For example, while the arithmetic average monthly return of the benchmark was 2.0 percent, the mean gross monthly return of investors was just 0.5 percent. And over 75 percent of investors underperformed.
- People overrate themselves. Only 30 percent considered themselves to be average. Investors overestimated their own performance by an astounding 11.6 percent a year. And portfolio performance was negatively related with the absolute difference between return estimates and realized returns—the lower the returns, the worse investors were when judging their realized returns. It seems likely that investors are unable to admit how badly they have done. In fact, while just 5 percent believed they had experienced negative returns, the reality was that 25 percent did so.

At this point, you should be asking yourself the following questions: "Do I know the rate of return on each of my investments and my portfolio as a whole?" and "Do I know how the returns compared to the returns of appropriate benchmarks?"

If you are like the typical investor, you are unlikely to have the correct answers. And that is not a good thing because it is impossible to judge the success of a strategy without knowing the answers to these questions.

Admissions from Industry Practitioners

In a 2004 interview with *Wall Street Journal* reporter Jon E. Hilsenrath, Richard Thaler conceded that most of his retirement assets were held in index funds. He also conceded that "it is not easy to beat the market, and most people don't."[4]

Richard Roll is a professor of finance at UCLA's Anderson School of Management. He was also a vice president at Goldman Sachs, where he founded the mortgage securities research group in 1985. His 1968 doctoral thesis won the Irving Fisher Prize as the best American dissertation in economics. He has won the Graham and Dodd Award for financial writing three times and the Leo Melamed Award for the best financial research by an American business school professor. He is a past president of the American Finance Association and has been an associate editor of 11 different journals in finance and economics. And he is a principal in the firm Roll and Ross Asset Management. Pay careful attention to his admission:

> I have personally tried to invest money, my client's and my own, in every single anomaly and predictive result that academics have dreamed up. And I have yet to make a nickel on any of these supposed market inefficiencies. An inefficiency ought to be an exploitable opportunity. If there's nothing investors can exploit in a systematic way, time in and time out, then it's very hard to say that information is not being properly incorporated into stock prices. Real money investment strategies don't produce the results that academic papers say they should.[5]

Summary

You have now seen the evidence on attempts to generate persistent alpha by mutual funds, pension plans, hedge funds, venture capitalists, individual investors, and behavioral finance practitioners. The evidence is so overwhelming that the only conclusions that can be drawn are:

- The markets are highly efficient, or
- The costs of exploiting any inefficiencies are sufficiently great to make it difficult to generate persistent alpha sufficient to overcome the costs of the efforts, and
- If there are inefficiencies, the competition to exploit them causes them to disappear rapidly. This is a subject we will explore in the next chapter.

Chapter 7

Why Persistent Outperformance Is Hard to Find

A s you have seen, there is an overwhelming body of evidence that the quest for the Holy Grail of alpha has been a dismal failure, costing investors tens of billions of dollars each year. An interesting question is: why has the quest failed when it seems logical that those with above-average skills should produce above-average results?

After all, it is true in virtually every other endeavor. To quote my ex-boss: "Diligence, hard work, research, and intelligence just have to pay off in superior results. How can no management be better than professional management?"

As you will see, the problem with this thought process is that, while these statements are correct generalizations, efforts to beat the market are an exception to the rule. The focus of this chapter is to explain why there is no evidence of any persistent ability to produce alpha beyond the randomly expected.

The Quest for Alpha Is a Game Played on a Different Field

Roger Federer is the greatest tennis player of his era and perhaps the greatest ever. No one would consider it luck that he won a record 15 Grand Slam singles titles. He is so persistently outstanding that he reached the semifinals of 23 consecutive Grand Slams—more than doubling the previous record.

What is important to understand is that Federer's competition is other *individual* players. In terms of individual skills, Andy Roddick has a better serve, Andy Murray has a better backhand, Fernando Gonzalez has a better forehand, Rafael Nadal has a better baseline game and is considered a superior player on clay, Radek Stepanek has a better net game, and David Ferrer is faster. Yet, Federer is the best player.

The world of investing presents a different situation. The difference is why we don't see persistence of outperformance of investment managers. To understand the difference, we need to understand how securities markets set prices.

Dr. Mark Rubinstein (professor of applied investment analysis, University of California, Berkeley, Haas School of Business) provided the following insight:

> Each investor, using the market to serve his or her own self-interest, unwittingly makes prices reflect that investor's information and analysis. It is as if the market were a huge, relatively low-cost, continuous polling mechanism that records the updated votes of millions of investors in continuously changing current prices. In light of this mechanism, for a single investor (in the absence of inside information) to believe that prices are significantly in error is almost always folly. Public information should already be embedded in prices.[1]

Rubinstein is making the point that the competition for an investment manager is not other individual investment managers, but is instead the *collective wisdom* of the market—Adam Smith's famous "invisible hand." As author Ron Ross points out in *The Unbeatable Market*: "The quest for market-beating strategy boils down to an information-processing contest. The entity you are competing against is the *entire* market and the accumulated information discovered by all the participants and reflected in prices."[2]

Here is another way to think about the quest for superior investment performance: "The potential for self-cancellation shows why the game of investing is so different from, for example, chess, in which even a seemingly small advantage can lead to consistent victories. Investors implicitly lump the market with other arenas of competition in their experience."[3] Rex Sinquefield, former co-chairman of DFA, put it this way: "Just because there are some investors smarter than others, that advantage will not show up. The market is too vast and too informationally efficient."[4]

While the competition for Roger Federer is other individual players, the competition for investment managers is the entire market. It would be as if each time Federer stepped on the court he faced an opponent with Andy Roddick's serve, Andy Murray's backhand, Rafael Nadal's baseline game, and so on. If that had been the case, Federer would not have produced the same results.

It is important to understand that the results of any game are more dependent on the skill level of the competition than on the skill of the individual competing. In the world of investing, the competition is indeed tough. With as much as 80 to 90 percent of the trading done by institutional investors, it is difficult to think of a large enough group of victims to exploit in order to generate alpha, especially after considering the costs of the efforts—bringing us to the next important point.

When Federer plays tennis, he is engaged in a zero-sum game—either he wins the match or his opponent does. Investment managers trying to outperform are not engaged in a zero-sum game. Their quest for alpha generates incremental expenses. Those costs include research expenses, other fund expenses, bid-offer spreads, commissions, market impact costs, and taxes (for taxable accounts). It would be as if each time Federer stepped on the court, he wore a pair of ankle weights while his opponent had no such handicap.

Peter Bernstein, author of several highly regarded investment books including *Against the Gods* and *Capital Ideas*, observed: "In the real world, investors seem to have great difficulty outperforming one another in any convincing or consistent fashion. Today's hero is often tomorrow's blockhead."[5]

To avoid choosing the wrong strategy, one must understand the nature of the game. In the investment arena, large institutional investors dominate trading. They are the ones setting prices. Thus, the competition is extremely tough. Making the quest for alpha even more difficult is that the competition is not each individual institutional investor. Instead, it is the *collective wisdom* of all other participants. The competition is just too tough for it to be likely that any one investor will be able to persistently outperform.

The fact that the competition for alpha is extremely tough is not the only reason why the quest for the Holy Grail has failed.

Successful Active Management Sows the Seeds of Its Own Destruction

The Efficient Market Hypothesis (EMH) tells us that the lack of persistence of alpha should be expected. It is only by random good luck that a fund is able to outperform after the expenses of its efforts. There are also some very practical reasons why even the most successful active funds seem to lose their luster over time. Let's examine why even the most successful funds contain the seeds of their own destruction. In fact, the more successful the fund is, the more likely it is that its outperformance will be "gone with the wind."

Fund managers know that the more a fund diversifies, the more it looks and performs like its benchmark index. (A fund whose holdings are very similar to those of its benchmark is known as a *closet index* fund.) To have the greatest chance to outperform, a fund must concentrate its assets in a few stocks (which is why focus funds were created). While a strategy of owning just a few of a manager's best ideas is the most likely way to generate world-class returns, it is also the most likely way to end up at the bottom of the rankings list.

Let's look at how the mutual fund world works. A new fund is created. The fund starts out with a very small amount of assets under management. Aware of the risks of being a closet indexer (we will cover this issue shortly), the fund concentrates its assets in just a few stocks. The fund also knows that the market for large caps is highly efficient in terms of information. Therefore, it concentrates its research efforts in the less efficient (at least in terms of information) asset class of small-cap stocks. The fund must comply with the Securities and Exchange Commission's (SEC's) rules on diversification—it cannot have more than 5 percent of its assets in any one stock. The fund happens to be in the right place at the right time, or has one of the very rare, truly gifted managers—the next Peter Lynch—and earns spectacular returns for a few years. The fund is given the coveted five-star rating from Morningstar and starts to advertise its great performance. Assets come rushing in. The better the performance, the more money pours in. The fund is now faced with a dilemma. It can buy ever-larger positions in just a few small-cap stocks, it can increase its diversification, or it can style drift to large-cap stocks. Each course contains the seeds of the fund's likely future inability to persist with its track record of outperformance. Let's see why. We begin by considering the alternative of diversifying holdings.

Closet Indexing

If a fund starts to diversify and buys the stocks of more small companies, it runs into the mathematics of "closet indexing." A closet index fund looks like an actively managed fund, but the stocks it owns so closely resemble the holdings of an index fund that investors are unknowingly paying very large fees for minimal differentiation. For example, if we assume that a fund is even as much as 50 percent differentiated from its benchmark index, the hurdle created by the operating expense ratio is twice the difference between its expense ratio and the expense ratio of the benchmark index fund. If the fund is only 20 percent differentiated, the hurdle becomes five times the difference in the operating expense ratios.

A relatively good indicator of the amount of differentiation is the actively managed fund's correlation with its benchmark index (such as the S&P 500 Index for large-cap stocks or the S&P 600 Index for small-cap stocks). The higher the correlation—measured by a fund's r, or the correlation coefficient—the less likely the differentiation will be. The r-squared $(r \times r)$, or the coefficient of determination, is commonly used to measure the degree of differentiation compared to a benchmark. Remember that the larger the fund, the more diversified it will likely become. The more it diversifies, the greater becomes its r-squared and the greater the hurdle the manager must overcome to outperform. Add this hurdle to the other expenses that actively managed funds and their investors must overcome (bid/offer spreads, commissions, market impact costs, the drag of cash, and taxes for taxable accounts), and the hurdle becomes almost insurmountable.

The following is evidence of the difficulty of overcoming a high r-squared, given the greater fees and the other expenses incurred by active managers. A study found that for the three years ending August 31, 1999, the five largest funds with r-squared over 0.95 returned between 21 and 26.9 percent. An investor would have received between 18 and 24.6 percent after taxes. Vanguard's 500 Index fund beat them all. It returned 28.5 percent pretax and 27.5 percent after tax. Of the 80 largest funds with r-squared over 0.95, only three managed to beat the Vanguard 500 Index Fund, and they just barely did so. And none did so after taxes.[6] That accounted for about $400 billion of underperforming assets.

Concentration and the Role of Trading Costs

The second alternative to dealing with cash inflows is to concentrate assets in the same few stocks. Here the fund runs into the problem of market impact costs. Market impact occurs when a mutual fund buys or sells a large block of stock. The fund's purchases or sales cause the stock to move beyond its current bid (lower) or offer (higher) price, increasing the cost of trading.

The research organization Barra has studied market impact costs. While the cost of market impact will vary depending on many factors (such as fund size, asset class, turnover) the cost can be quite substantial. Barra noted that a fairly typical small- or mid-cap stock fund with $500 million in assets and an annual turnover rate of between 80 and 100 percent could lose 3 to 5 percent per annum to market impact costs—far more than the annual expenses of most funds. Because of lack of liquidity, the smaller the market capitalization, the greater the market impact cost. And the larger the fund, the greater the market impact costs become. Even large-cap funds can have large market impact costs, as illustrated by the 8.13 percent figure Barra estimated for the Phoenix Engemann Aggressive Growth Fund.[7]

The Role of Trading Costs

The 2007 study "Scale Effects in Mutual Fund Performance: The Role of Trading Costs" provided evidence supporting the findings of the Barra study. The authors examined the role of trading costs as a source of diseconomies of scale for mutual funds. They studied the annual trading costs for 1,706 U.S. equity funds during the period 1995–2005 and found:

- Trading costs for mutual funds are on average even greater in magnitude than the expense ratio.
- The variation in returns is related to fund trade size.
- Annual trading costs bear a statistically significant negative relation to performance.
- Trading has an increasingly detrimental impact on performance as a fund's relative trade size increases.
- Trading fails to recover its costs—$1 in trading costs reduced fund assets by $0.41. However, while trading does not adversely impact performance at funds with a relatively small average trade size, trading costs *decrease* fund assets by roughly $0.80 for funds that have large average trades.
- Flow-driven trades are shown to be significantly more costly than discretionary trades. Flow-driven trades are those created by investors' additions to and withdrawals from a fund. This nondiscretionary trade motive partially— but not fully—explains the negative impact of trading on performance.

- Relative trade size subsumes fund size in regressions of fund returns. Thus, trading costs are likely to be the primary source of diseconomies of scale for funds.

The authors concluded: "Our evidence directly establishes scale effects in trading as a source of diminishing returns to scale from active management."[8]

There is a third alternative that many mutual funds will follow because it allows funds to avoid the market impact costs that concentration creates.

Drifting Out of Small Caps

The third alternative to closet indexing and continued concentration is to start buying larger-cap stocks. The problem here is that the larger the market cap, the more efficient the market is in terms of information. This makes it extremely difficult to outperform. One example of the likelihood of failure is that for the decade of the 1980s, only two large-cap growth funds that even survived the entire decade managed to outperform the Vanguard 500 Index Fund after taxes.[9]

No matter which way the manager turns, the likelihood of continued outperformance diminishes. The alternative is to stay small in terms of assets. This can be accomplished by closing the fund to new investors. The problem here is that not many funds are willing to forgo the profits from increased assets under management.

Encore Performances

John Bogle studied the encore performances of top performing actively managed funds. His findings support the theory (along with the Efficient Market Hypothesis [EMH] which states that success was a function of a random outcome) that successful performance contains the seeds of its own destruction.[10] Bogle compared the performance of the top 20 funds of the period 1972–1982 with their performance for the period 1982–1992. He found that the top 20 funds did perform slightly better in the second period than the average active fund, finishing in the 54th percentile. However, the margin of outperformance fell from 8.3 percent to just 1.2 percent. More importantly, they *underperformed* the S&P 500 by 1.8 percent—and that is before considering any loads or the impact of taxes. One further point: The dispersion of returns in the succeeding period was huge—rankings ranged from two to 245 (out of 309). Investors might have gotten lucky, or they might have paid a big price. There was no way to know before the fact.

Bogle found a similar story when he examined returns for the periods 1982–1992 and 1992–September 30, 2001. The top 20 performers from the first period finished the succeeding period with an average ranking at the 58th percentile. However, the average outperformance fell from 4.9 percent to just 0.9 percent. More importantly, they *underperformed* the S&P 500 by 1.5 percent. Again, this is before considering any loads or the impact of taxes. Also, once again, there was a wide dispersion of returns—rankings ranged from 14 to 823 (out of 841). Again, lots of unnecessary risk. Simply accepting market returns would have delivered above average performance.

There is yet a further problem for active management. Since it takes time before a manager demonstrates top performance, most of the outperformance will likely occur when the fund's assets are very small. Very few shareholders actually earn the great returns. Most fund assets come piling in only *after* great returns are earned. When the fund's performance reverts to the mean (which is what the evidence suggests is highly likely to occur), despite the fact that the fund may still show outperformance, most of a fund's invested dollars may earn below-benchmark returns. As we have seen, by chasing yesterday's returns, investors earn rates of return well below those of the very funds in which they invest. They tend to buy high (*after* great performance), and sell low (*after* poor performance). Not exactly a prescription for successful investing.

Who Gets the Money to Manage?

To complete our story on why persistent alpha is so hard to find, we turn to Jonathan Berk (professor of finance, University of California, Berkeley). Berk suggests asking: "Who gets money to manage? Since investors have access to databases that provide returns histories, and everyone wants to have their money managed by the best manager, money will flow to the best manager first. Eventually, the best manager will receive so much money that it will impact his ability to generate superior returns and his expected return will be driven down to the second best manager's expected return. At that point investors will be indifferent to investing with either manager, and so funds will flow to both managers until their expected returns are driven down to the third best manager. This process will continue until the expected return of investing with any manager is the benchmark expected return—the return investors can expect to receive by investing in a passive strategy of similar riskiness. At that point investors are indifferent between investing with active managers or just indexing and an equilibrium is achieved." [11]

Berk went on to point out that the manager with the most skill ends up with the most money. He added: "When capital is supplied competitively by investors but ability is scarce, only participants with the skill in short supply can earn economic rents. Investors who choose to invest with active managers cannot expect to receive positive excess returns on a risk-adjusted basis. If they did, there would be an excess supply of capital to those managers."[12]

This is an important insight. Just as the EMH explains why investors cannot use publicly available information to beat the market (because all investors have access to that information and it is, therefore, already embedded in prices), the same is true of active managers. Investors should not expect to outperform the market by using publicly available information to select active managers. Any excess return should go to the active manager (in the form of higher expenses).

The process is simple. Investors observe benchmark-beating performance and funds flow into the top performers. And as we have seen, the investment inflow eliminates return persistence because fund managers face diminishing returns to scale.

The study "Performance Persistence in Institutional Investment Management" provides further support for Berk's hypothesis. The authors investigated the relationship between performance and flows across portfolios in each of the three asset classes—domestic equities, international equities and fixed income. Avoiding survivorship bias, the study examined performance persistence in 6,027 institutional portfolios managed by 1,475 investment management firms between 1991 and 2004. The following is a summary of their findings:[13]

- Unlike retail mutual funds, persistence in winner domestic equity portfolios was significant and economically large for up to one year. This difference is explained by the fact that retail investors incur little to no costs (at least in tax-advantaged accounts) to transition from one fund/manager to another. Thus, in retail mutual funds, redemptions and capital inflows are rapid. In contrast, in an institutional setting, capital flows are sticky because transaction costs from exiting one portfolio and entering a new one are large and potentially prohibitive. As a result, the equilibration process for institutional fund managers takes longer.

- Eventually, capital flows follow performance. Capital flows for domestic equity portfolios one year after portfolio formation increased monotonically from loser to winner deciles. The spread in flows between the extreme winner and loser deciles was as much as 36 percent of total net assets. Similar results were found for fixed income and international equity portfolios.

- Top performers draw an influx of assets from plan sponsors. The large capital inflows had severe consequences for future performance. In the year following such inflows, alphas sharply declined. There is a strong negative relationship between incremental flows and future performance, especially among larger funds. After the first year, domestic and international equity alphas were statistically indistinguishable from zero even before fees. Similar results were found for fixed income portfolios, once an adjustment was made to address high-yield assets.

We continue our discussion on why persistent alpha is so hard to find by looking at the evidence on the value of economic and market forecasts.

The Value of Economic and Market Forecasts

The underlying basis for most stock market forecasts is an economic forecast. The question is: do economic forecasts have any value? William Sherden provided us with the answer.

Sherden is an adjunct professor at the Stanford Business School. He is also the author of a book I highly recommend, *The Fortune Sellers*. In 1985, when preparing testimony as an expert witness, Sherden analyzed the track records of inflation projections by different forecasting methods. He compared those forecasts to what is called the "naive" forecast—simply projecting today's inflation rate into the future. He was surprised to learn that the simple naive forecast proved to be the most accurate, beating the forecasts of the most prestigious economic forecasting firms equipped with PhDs from leading universities and thousand-equation computer models.

Sherden then reviewed the leading research on forecasting accuracy from 1979 to 1995 and forecasts made from 1970 to 1995. He concluded that:

- *Economists cannot predict the turning points in the economy.* Of the 48 predictions made by economists, 46 missed the turning points.
- *Economists' forecasting skill is about as good as guessing.* For example, even the economists who directly or indirectly run the economy—the Federal Reserve, the Council of Economic Advisors, and the Congressional Budget Office—had forecasting records that were worse than pure chance.
- *There are no economic forecasters who consistently lead the pack in forecasting accuracy.*
- *There are no economic ideologies whose adherents produce consistently superior economic forecasts.*
- *Increased sophistication provides no improvement in economic forecasting accuracy.*
- *Consensus forecasts offer little improvement.*
- *Forecasts may be affected by psychological bias.* Some economists are perpetually optimistic and others perpetually pessimistic.[14]

Perhaps the most damaging of Sherden's findings was that economists do not provide accurate forecasts when accuracy is most important—at the turning points of the economy. While it might make little difference if you forecast a growth rate of 3 percent and it turns out to be 2 or 4 percent, it certainly makes a difference if you forecast continued economic growth and we are headed into a recession, or if you forecast a continuing recession and the economy is set to turn around.

The 2009 study "How Accurate Are Forecasts in a Recession" by Federal Reserve Bank of St. Louis economist Michael W. McCracken, provided further evidence on the failure of economic forecasters to get it right when it is most important.[15] Using as his database the Survey of Professional Forecasters (SPF), McCracken reviewed 26 years of quarterly, one-year-ahead mean SPF forecasts from the third quarter of 1981 through the third quarter of 2007. He found that forecaster errors were four times larger when the economy was in recession than when it was not. Just when you would like to know when it is safe to buy stocks again, forecasting skill (which is not good to begin with) deteriorates significantly.

Since the underlying basis of most stock market forecasts is an economic forecast, the evidence suggests that stock market strategists who predict bull and bear markets will have no greater success than do the economists.

William Sherden also made this important observation:

> Despite recent innovations in information technology and decades of academic research, successful stock market prediction has remained an elusive goal. In fact, the market is getting more complex and unpredictable as global trading brings in many new investors from numerous countries, computerized exchanges speed up transactions, and investors think up clever schemes to try to beat the market. Overall, we have not made progress in predicting the stock market, but this has not stopped the investment business from continuing the quest, and making $100 billion annually doing so.[16]

Sherden concluded by offering the following advice (with which I wholeheartedly agree):

> Avoid market timers, for they promise something they cannot deliver. Cancel your subscription to market-timing newsletters. Tell the investment advisers selling the latest market-timing scheme to buzz off. Ignore news media predictions, since they haven't a clue as to what the market is going to do—although that will not stop them from publishing market predictions. Stop asking yourself and everyone you know, "What's the market going to do?" It is an irrelevant question, because it cannot be answered.[17]

Let's take a look at another study on the value of forecasts from so-called experts.

The Value of "Expert" Judgment

Philip E. Tetlock is a professor of psychology, business, and political science at the University of California, Berkeley and the author of *Expert Political Judgment: How Good Is It? How Can We Know?* The book provides the findings of his 20-year study in which experts were asked to predict the future.

Tetlock found that the so-called experts who make prediction their business—appearing as experts on television and talk radio, being quoted in the press, and advising governments and businesses—are no better than the proverbial chimps throwing darts.

Tetlock divided forecasters into two general categories: (1) foxes, who draw on a wide variety of experiences and for whom the world cannot be boiled down to a single idea; and (2) hedgehogs, who view the world through the lens of a single defining idea.

The following are some of his most interesting findings:[18]

- What distinguishes the worst forecasters from the not-so-bad is that while hedgehogs are more confident, they are wrong more often than foxes.
- What differentiates foxes from hedgehogs is that foxes rarely see things as bad as they appear at the trough or as good as they look at the peak.
- Optimists tend to be more accurate than pessimists.
- What experts think matters far less than how they think. We are better off turning to the foxes, who know many little things and accept ambiguity and contradiction as inevitable features of life, rather than turning to hedgehogs, who reach for formulaic solutions to ill-defined problems.
- It makes virtually no difference whether forecasters are PhDs, economists, political scientists, journalists, or historians; whether they had policy experience or access to classified information; or whether they had logged many or few years of experience in their chosen line of work. The only predictor of accuracy was fame, which was negatively correlated with accuracy: the most famous—those more likely feted by the media—made the worst forecasts.
- Beyond a stark minimum, subject matter expertise in world politics translates less into forecasting accuracy than it does into overconfidence and the ability to spin elaborate tapestries of reasons for expecting "favorite" outcomes.
- Like ordinary mortals, experts fall prey to the hindsight effect—they claim they knew more about what was going to happen than they actually knew before the fact. This systematic misremembering of past positions may look strategic, but the evidence indicates that people sometimes truly convince themselves that they "knew it all along."
- The "marketplace of ideas" can fail because consumers may be less interested in the dispassionate pursuit of truth than in buttressing their prejudices.

Tetlock also provided this important insight about hedge-hogs—they may be playing a different game. They are fighting to preserve their reputation in a cutthroat adversarial culture. They woo dumb-ass reporters who want glib sound bits. In their world, only the overconfident survive and only the truly arrogant thrive. He noted that the same self-assured hedgehog style of reasoning that suppresses forecasting accuracy and slows belief updating translates into attention-grabbing bold predictions that are rarely checked for accuracy.

Sadly, Tetlock concluded:

> No matter how unequivocal the evidence that experts cannot outpredict chimps or extrapolation algorithms, we should expect business to unfold as usual: pundits will continue to warn us on talk shows and op-ed pages of what will happen unless we dutifully follow their policy prescriptions. We, the consumers of expert pronouncements, are in thrall to experts for the same reasons that our ancestors submitted to shamans and oracles: our uncontrollable need to believe in a controllable world and have a flawed understanding of the laws of chance. We lack the will power and good sense to resist the snake oil products on offer. Who wants to believe that on the big questions we could do as well tossing a coin as by consulting accredited experts?

However, he noted that all is not lost:

> The fainthearted should be forgiven for concluding that we are fated to fail to break this tight symbiotic embrace between self-confident suppliers of dubious products and their cling-on customers. But even fierce resistance can be overcome. *Low-transaction-cost index funds have benefited—very substantially—from slowly spreading knowledge of how hard-pressed stock-pickers are to best dart-throwing chimps and other mindless algorithms.* [Emphasis mine]

The lesson Tetlock's research provides is that as much as we would like to believe there are those who can predict the future, prognosticating is the occupation of charlatans.

We All Want to Believe

In early 2009, I was in Baltimore giving a seminar for the invest-ment clients of a CPA firm. My talk was called "The Winning Investment Strategy." The talk focused on the building of a globally diversified portfolio of passively managed funds (such as index funds and exchange-traded funds) tailored to an indi-vidual's unique ability, willingness, and need to take risk. I also discussed the importance of integrating an investment plan into a well-developed estate, tax, and risk management (insurance of all types) plan. And I discussed the need to have the discipline to ignore all the economic and market forecasts that you hear from the financial media and Wall Street, which can lead you to aban-don your plan.

I explained that the reason you should ignore all eco-nomic and market forecasts is that the academic literature has concluded that there are no good economic and market fore-casters. I presented the aforementioned findings by Sherden as well as his recommendations. I also provided further support-ing evidence.

Despite my comments, the first question I received went like this: "What do you think is going to happen to the economy and the market over the next few months?" Since I always have an opinion (though I have learned never to act on my opinions, as they have no value), I was about to pro-vide it. But I caught myself and instead responded: "I would be happy to give you my opinion, but why would you care? I just explained that there are no good economic forecasters, and the right strategy is to ignore all of them and stick to your well-developed plan."

I continued: "I have served as an economist, run trad-ing rooms for major financial institutions, and provided economic forecasts to major corporations. When I got the forecast right, I would congratulate myself on how smart I was. When the forecast turned out wrong, I would blame it on bad luck—something happened that was impossible to have forecasted. Of course, if you keep doing that, at the end of the day you can call yourself a genius. I learned that it was always luck."

I also learned this important lesson. No matter how much we would like to believe otherwise, there is only one person who knows where the economy and the market are headed— and I don't get to talk to that person. And neither does anyone else, which is why one of my favorite quotations on the value of expert forecasts is: "No matter how much evidence exists that seers do not exist, suckers will pay for the existence of seers."[19]

In continuing our quest to understand why persistent alpha is so hard to find, we will consider a case study on the value of security analysis.

The Value of Security Analysis

As children we are taught that joy should come from the effort, not necessarily from the result. Not everyone can win the game, match, or race; climb to the top of the mountain; or finish a marathon. Hopefully, by the time we are adults, we have learned that lesson.

In contrast, one of the earliest lessons I learned in business was that, as a manager of people, I should never confuse efforts with results. Some employees delivered outstanding results with seemingly little effort. They worked a normal day, and their desks were never cluttered. They would take long lunch hours and would rarely seem harried. Sometimes they would come up with a single good idea that would provide great insights leading to improved profits. Other employees would put in a tremendous number of hours and were always busy, their desks swamped with piles of paper. Yet sometimes the results did not relate to the effort. In business, it is results that count, not effort. The same is true in the world of investing, because we cannot spend efforts, only returns.

The basic premise of active management is that security analysts are able to identify and purchase stocks that are undervalued and avoid stocks that are overvalued *through their efforts*. The *result* will be that investors who follow their recommendations will outperform the market. Is this premise myth or reality? The following example will help answer the question.

In May 1999, at a conference of financial economists at UCLA's Anderson School of Business, Bradford Cornell (professor emeritus, UCLA, Anderson School of Management) presented an example that provided insights into the value of the efforts of security analysts. As you will see, because much of the value of companies with high growth rates comes from distant cash flows, the value of their stock is highly sensitive to the size of the equity risk premium (ERP), the risk premium above the rate on riskless Treasury instruments that investors demand for accepting the risks of equity ownership. In 1999, Intel was certainly considered a company with expectations for a high rate of growth.

Intel had accumulated over $10 billion of cash. The board of directors was trying to determine if it made sense to use a substantial portion of the cash to repurchase its stock. At the time, the stock was trading at about $120 per share. Based on publicly available forecasts of future cash flows, Cornell demonstrated that if the ERP were 3 percent, Intel's stock would be worth $204. If the ERP were 5 percent, the stock would be worth $130 (about the current price). And if the ERP were 7.2 percent, the stock would be worth just $82.

Buy, Sell, or Hold?

With such a wide range of estimated values, what should the board do? If the stock was worth $204, they should begin an aggressive repurchase program. However, if it was worth $82, they should take advantage of the current "overvaluation" and raise capital by issuing more shares. The board was faced with two problems. The first was that the valuations assumed that the cash flow projections were *known*. Not even the board (let alone some security analyst) can see the future with such clarity. Obviously, in the real world we can only make estimates of future cash flows. The second problem is: Why would the board believe that it could predict the ERP any better than the market could? And you see how much the valuation changes with changes in the ERP.

The board decided not to take any action. With the benefit of hindsight, they would have been best served to issue more shares as the stock collapsed in 2000 and has yet to recover to anywhere near $120.

If corporate insiders, with access to far more information than any security analyst is likely to possess, have such great difficulty in determining a "correct" valuation, it is easy to understand why the results of conventional stock-picking methods (active management) are poor and inconsistent. While security analysts and active portfolio managers are putting forth great effort in attempts to beat the market, the historical evidence is that the majority of the time, those efforts prove counterproductive.

James Lorie was a professor of finance at the Graduate School of Business at the University of Chicago. With Mary Hamilton, he co-authored the book *The Stock Market: Theories and Evidence*. Regarding the value of security analysis, they observed:

The most general implication of the efficient market hypothesis is that most security analysis is logically incomplete and value-less. . . . The logical incompleteness consists of failing to determine or even consider whether the price of the stock already reflects the substance of the analysis. A very optimistic forecast of a company's future earnings is no justification for buying the stock. Such marked differences of opinion are the basis of abnormal gains and losses. A proper analytical report will include evidence of the existence of such a difference and support for the analyst's own view.[20]

The Hurdles Are Getting Higher

As you have seen, the historical evidence that passive investing is the prudent strategy is compelling. If we examine trends in information, communications, trading costs, and institutional ownership, it will be clear that the hurdles for active management are getting ever higher.

In an article titled "Are Active Management Fees Too High?," Richard Ennis provided the following insights.[21]

Information

Market efficiency depends on information being available to the public. The arrival of the Internet and high-speed computers provides greater access to information and the ability to rapidly analyze it. In addition, the SEC's implementation of the fair disclosure rule reduces the potential for selective distribution of information.

Communications

Market efficiency also depends on participants having rapid access to information. Today, with the Internet and Blackberries, information is both virtually instantaneous and cheap.

Trading Costs

If trading costs are high, there can be impediments to trading, creating opportunities for mispricing. With the advent of electronic exchanges, bid-offer spreads and trading costs have fallen. In addition, the technological innovations in derivative securities and the advent of exchange-traded funds have lowered the costs of trading and improved the ability to hedge risks. And low-cost brokerage firms have lowered the cost of commissions for individual investors.

Institutional Ownership

Since outperforming the market before expenses is a zero-sum game (for every winner there is a loser), to outperform there must be victims to exploit. As we have discussed, stocks that individual investors buy underperform after they buy them and stocks they sell outperform after they sell them. Since for every loser there must be a winner, on average, institutional investors are exploiting individual investors whenever they trade. Fifty years ago, perhaps as little as 10 percent of shares were held by institutional investors. Thus, there were plenty of victims to exploit. Today, it is estimated that as much as 80 to 90 percent of all trading is done by institutional investors—including thousands of hedge funds. Thus, the competition has gotten tougher. Through their trading activities, these funds serve to make the markets more efficient. It doesn't appear that there are enough victims to exploit.

Advice from Professional Investors and Academics

Benjamin Graham is probably our most famous and most highly revered investor. He is considered the father of the value style of investing. He co-authored the bestseller *Security*

Analysis. Graham taught his theories at Columbia University. Warren Buffett credits Graham for grounding him with a sound intellectual investment framework. He described Graham as the second most influential person in his life after his own father and named his son Howard Graham Buffett. At the end of his illustrious career, Graham offered this advice: "If I have noticed anything over these 60 years on Wall Street, it is that people do not succeed in forecasting what's going to happen to the stock market."[22]

William Sherden offered this advice:

> Remember the First Law of Economics: For every economist, there is an equal and opposite economist—so for every bullish economist, there is a bearish one. The Second Law of Economics: They are both likely to be wrong.[23]

Stephen Gould was one of America's most prominent scientists and one of our most widely read writers of popular science. He taught at both Harvard and NYU. Gould offered investors this advice:

> Probably more intellectual energy has been invested in discovering (and exploiting) trends in the stock market than in any other subject—for the obvious reason that stakes are so high, as measured in the currency of our culture. The fact that no one has ever come close to finding a consistent way to beat the system—despite intense efforts by some of the smartest people in the world—probably indicates that such causal trends do not exist, and that sequences are effectively random.[24]

Fischer Black was one of our most famous economists, best known as the co-author of the Black-Scholes option-pricing model. It is likely that he would have been awarded the Nobel Prize in economics, but it is not awarded posthumously. In 2002, the American Finance Association established the Fischer Black Prize. The award is given to a young researcher whose body of work "best exemplifies the Fischer Black hallmark of

developing original research that is relevant to finance practice." Black, in an interview with Roger Ibbotson, offered this
advice: "Information is more valuable sold than used."[25]

Nobel Prize winner Merton Miller offered this advice in
an interview with *Barron's:*

> "Don't quote me on this, but I'd say don't read *Barron's* . . . because
> it will only tease you about investment opportunities that you'd
> best avoid."[26]

Paul Samuelson was a Nobel Laureate in economics. He
offered this perspective on the value of portfolio managers:

> [A] respect for evidence compels me to incline toward the hypoth-
> esis that most portfolio decision makers should go out of business—
> take up plumbing, teach Greek, or help produce the annual GNP
> by serving as corporate executives. Even if this advice to drop dead
> is good advice, it obviously is not counsel that will be eagerly fol-
> lowed. Few people will commit suicide without a push.[27]

Warren Buffett offered this advice: "A prediction about the
direction of the stock market tells you nothing about where
stocks are headed, but a whole lot about the person doing the
predicting."[28]

Admissions from Industry Practitioners and Academics

John Kenneth Galbraith was one of our most famous econ-
omists. He was a professor of economics at Harvard and
served as president of the American Economic Association.
Galbraith also served in the administrations of Franklin Delano
Roosevelt, Harry Truman, John F. Kennedy, and Lyndon
Johnson. From 1943 until 1948, he served as editor of *Fortune*.
His books on economic topics were bestsellers from the 1950s
through the 1970s. Commenting on the ability of economic

forecasters, Galbraith stated: "We have two classes of forecasters: those who don't know—and those who don't know they don't know."[29]

I would add a third class, the one that probably constitutes the majority: those who know they don't know but get paid a lot of money to pretend they do.

The following quotation is particularly insightful since it came from Michael Evans, who at the time was chairman of Chase Econometrics (now known as IHS Global Insight): "The trouble with macro [economic] forecasting is that no one can do it."[30]

IHS Global Insight's web site (www.globalinsight.com) declares: "IHS Global Insight is the world leader in economic and financial analysis, forecasting and market intelligence with more than 40 years' experience and an outstanding record for accuracy." The firm probably collects tens of millions of dollars for providing insights on what Evans admitted no one can do.

Barton Biggs was the chief global strategist for Morgan Stanley. He was named by *Institutional Investor* magazine to its All-America Research Team 10 times, and he was voted the top global strategist and first in global asset allocation from 1996 to 2000 by the magazine's Investor Global Research Team poll.

Biggs appeared on the cover of a July 1993, issue of *Forbes* wearing a bear costume, warning investors: "We have all been spoiled by the 12 fat years we have just lived through." Convinced that the U.S. market had gotten way ahead of itself (meaning that investors were wrong to have bid the market up to such lofty levels), Biggs advised his clients to reduce their exposure to the U.S. market to 18 percent of their portfolio and to move their money overseas.

He argued that the U.S. market was near its top and was due for a fall that could range from 20 to 50 percent. "We're due for a secular bear market. It's been 20 years since the last one. Then, the decline could be 50 percent, as it was in the 1970s."

He added: "It doesn't take a genius to see that this relationship is due for a change."[31]

It took almost seven years before the bear market Biggs called for finally arrived. During this period, the United States experienced its greatest bull market ever (one that Mr. Biggs's clients presumably missed out on). In addition, despite his claim that "it doesn't take a genius to see that this relationship is due for a change," the U.S market far outperformed the European and emerging-country markets—markets in which Mr. Biggs was advising his clients to invest—by margins of about two to one.

Perhaps this incident led Biggs to admit: "God made global strategists so weathermen would look good."[32]

Gary Shilling is an economist and the president of A. Gary Shilling & Co., Inc. and editor of *A. Gary Shilling's Insight*. He is a regular contributor to such publications as *Forbes*, the *New York Times,* and the *Wall Street Journal*. He frequently appears on CNBC. Here is what he had to say on the value of forecasts: "Hollywood producers with all their market research dollars get paid zillions of dollars and they don't get it right. Why should I, a mere economist, think I can do any better?"[33]

Joseph Mezrich was the head of Quantitative Strategies Group at Morgan Stanley Dean Witter when he admitted, "Surprise is a persistently important factor in stock performance."[34]

This admission is of great importance. The dictionary defines *surprise* as causing an effect through being unexpected at a particular time or place. And since surprise is a persistently important factor in stock performance, efforts to outperform the market by actively managed funds are likely to prove futile. The logic is simple. First, if there are no surprises in terms of new information, the market will have already incorporated the expected results into prices. However, if the new information is a surprise, by definition the impact of the new information is not predictable (it is a surprise). Bottom line: the effect of surprises on market prices may be explainable but not exploitable.

Charles Clough was chief market strategist for Merrill Lynch when he stated: "I'm the lousiest market timer in the history of the world."[35]

Personal finance columnist Jason Zweig offered this advice:

> The ancient Scythians discouraged frivolous prophecies by burning to death any soothsayer whose predictions failed to come true. . . . Investors might be better off if modern forms of divination like market forecasts and earnings projections were held to biblical standards of justice.[36]

John Liscio wrote and published the financial newsletter *The Liscio Report*. In an interview with *Barron's*, Liscio stated: "I don't try to forecast. I don't think forecasting is something within the realm of human possibility."[37]

Fred Henning was the head of fixed income investing at Fidelity Investments when he made this astonishing admission: "Basically, we were guessing on interest rates. . . . What we've come to believe is that no one can guess interest rates."[38]

Fidelity was happy to charge high fees for Henning's guesses. Investors, however, would probably not have been happy to know they were paying for nothing more than guesses.

Ben Bernanke is the chairman of the Federal Reserve. He advises skepticism about the ability to foretell the future:

> As an economist and policymaker, I have plenty of experience in trying to foretell the future, because policy decisions inevitably involve projections of how alternative policy choices will influence the future course of the economy. The Federal Reserve, therefore, devotes substantial resources to economic forecasting. Likewise, individual investors and businesses have strong financial incentives to try to anticipate how the economy will evolve. With so much at stake, you will not be surprised to know that, over the years, many very smart people have applied the most sophisticated

statistical and modeling tools available to try to better divine the economic future. But the results, unfortunately, have more often than not been underwhelming. Like weather forecasters, economic forecasters must deal with a system that is extraordinarily complex, that is subject to random shocks, and about which our data and understanding will always be imperfect. In some ways, predicting the economy is even more difficult than forecasting the weather, because the economy is not made up of molecules whose behavior is subject to the laws of physics, but rather of human beings who are themselves thinking about the future and whose behavior may be influenced by the forecasts that they or others make. To be sure, historical relationships and regularities can help economists, as well as weather forecasters, gain some insight into the future, but these must be used with considerable caution and healthy skepticism.[39]

A fitting conclusion to this chapter is this tale of three "city slickers." Each year, three friends—a doctor, a lawyer, and a market strategist—went on an adventure. This year, they decided to travel to the mountains of Colorado to whitewater raft, climb mountains, hot air balloon, and visit some of the old mining towns. While out hiking in the mountains, the sky turned ominously dark. Totally unprepared for this eventuality, they started to panic.

The lawyer remembered that they had passed a farmhouse a couple of miles back and recommended they head for it as quickly as possible. Luckily, they made it just before torrential rain began to pour down. They knocked on the door, and a farmer greeted them. They explained their predicament and asked if the farmer could provide shelter for the evening. The farmer explained he would be glad to but he only had room in the house for two. The third would have to sleep in the barn with his animals. The doctor, having grown up on a farm, volunteered to sleep in the barn. The farmer gave him a pillow, some blankets, and an umbrella and sent him on his way.

Two minutes later, there was a knock on the door. Standing there was the doctor.

The farmer asked: "What's the matter?" The doctor replied: "I am a Hindu. In my religion, cows are sacred animals. I did not know there were cows in the barn. I cannot sleep with cows."

The lawyer volunteered to take his place. Two minutes passed. Then the lawyer knocked on the door.

The farmer asked, "What's the matter now?" The lawyer explained that he was Jewish, and pigs are not kosher animals. He could not sleep with pigs.

So the market strategist agreed to sleep in the barn. Two minutes later, there was another knock on the door. The farmer swung open the door for the third time. Standing on the front porch were the cows, the pigs, the chickens, and the horses.

Chapter 8

The Prudent Investor Rule

C hapters 1 through 6 presented the evidence that demonstrates the quest for the Holy Grail of alpha has been about as successful as the quests of Percival and Galahad. They also presented the advice against pursuing the Holy Grail of alpha from legendary investors such as Benjamin Graham, Peter Lynch, and Warren Buffett, as well as from leading academics. And you read the admissions of industry practitioners and members of the financial media. Chapter 7 presented the evidence on why persistent alpha is so hard to find and why market and economic forecasts are best ignored. It also presented advice and comments from practioners and academics.

There is one more story we need to cover about market efficiency. It is an old joke about a financial economist who was a passionate defender of the Efficient Market Hypothesis (EMH). He was walking down the street with a friend. The friend stops and says: "Look! There is a $20 bill on the ground." The economist turns and says: "Can't be. If there were a $20 bill on the ground, somebody would have already picked it up."

This joke is told by those who believe that the markets are inefficient and that investors can outperform the market by exploiting mispricings—finding an undervalued stock instead of a $20 bill. It is important to understand that this is a misleading analogy to the EMH. The following version of the story is a more accurate one.

A financial economist and passionate defender of the EMH was walking down the street with a friend. The friend stops and says: "Look! There is a $20 bill on the ground." The economist turns and says: "Boy, this must be our lucky day! Better pick it up quick because the market is so efficient it won't be there for long. Finding a $20 bill lying around happens so infrequently it would be foolish to spend our time searching for more of them. Certainly, after assigning a value to the time spent in the effort, an 'investment' in trying to find money lying on the street just waiting to be picked up would be a poor one. I am certainly not aware of anyone who has obtained their wealth by 'mining' beaches with metal detectors." When he had finished, they both looked down, and the $20 bill was gone.

There is also what might be called the "Hollywood version" of this story. A financial economist and passionate defender of the EMH was walking down the street with a friend. The friend stops and says: "Look! There is a $20 bill on the ground." The economist turns and says: "Can't be. If there were a $20 bill on the ground, somebody would have already picked it up." The friend picks up the $20 bill and dashes off. Deciding this is an easy way to make a living, he abandons his job and begins to search the world for $20 bills lying on the ground waiting to be picked up.

A year later, the economist is walking down the same street and sees his long-lost friend sitting on the sidewalk wearing torn and filthy clothing. Appalled to see the disheveled state into which his friend has sunk, he rushes over to find out what happened. The friend tells him that he never found another $20 bill on the ground.

Those that tell the first version of the story fail to understand that an efficient market doesn't mean that there cannot be a $20 bill waiting to be found. Instead, it means that it is so unlikely that you will find one that it does not pay to go looking for them—the costs of the effort are likely to exceed the benefits. In addition, if it became known that there were lots of $20 bills to be found in a certain area, everyone would be there competing to find them. That reduces the likelihood of achieving an appropriate "return on investment."

The analogy to the EMH is that it is not impossible to uncover an anomaly (the $20 bill on the street) that can be exploited (being able to buy a stock that is somehow undervalued by the market). Instead, one of the fundamental tenets of the EMH is that successful trading strategies self-destruct in a competitive financial environment because they are self-limiting— when they are discovered, they are eliminated by the very act of exploiting the anomaly.

Economics professors Dwight Lee and James Verbrugge of the University of Georgia explain the power of the EMH in the following manner:

> The efficient market theory is practically alone among theories in that it becomes more powerful when people discover serious inconsistencies between it and the real world. If a clear efficient market anomaly is discovered, the behavior (or lack of behavior) that gives rise to it will tend to be eliminated by competition among investors for higher returns. . . .
>
> [For example] If stock prices are found to follow predictable seasonal patterns unrelated to financially relevant considerations, this knowledge will elicit responses that have the effect of eliminating the very patterns they were designed to exploit. . . .
>
> The implication here is rather striking. The more empirical flaws that are discovered in the efficient market theory, the more robust the theory becomes. . . .

[In effect] Those who do the most to ensure that the efficient market theory remains fundamental to our understanding of financial economics are not its intellectual defenders, but those mounting the most serious empirical assault against it.[1]

The Prudent Investor Rule

Embedded within the American legal code is a doctrine known as the Prudent Investor Rule. This rule requires those responsible for the management of someone else's assets to manage them in a manner appropriate to the financial circumstance and tolerance for risk of the beneficiaries as would a prudent investor. For example, if you are the trustee of the assets of an 83-year-old widow, you should be investing her money in safe assets, not in a hedge fund, venture capital, or emerging market bonds.

At one time, stocks were considered to be so risky that bonds were considered the only appropriate investments—even corporate pension funds reflected that view. That attitude has obviously changed. Equities are now considered appropriate investments (as long as the investment horizon is not short).

During the 1970s, pension fund sponsors began to discern that the collective performance of the active managers they hired to manage their pension fund assets was poor. This realization created the initial demand for index funds. Even though a few index funds became available, it wasn't until 1990 and the awarding of the Nobel Prize to Merton Miller, William Sharpe, and Harry Markowitz that the benefits of Modern Portfolio Theory (MPT) became more widely known.

The American Law Institute

According to its Web site, the American Law Institute (ALI) is the leading independent organization in the United States,

producing scholarly work to clarify, modernize, and otherwise
improve the law. The institute is made up of 4,000 lawyers,
judges, and law professors of the highest qualifications. It drafts,
discusses, revises, and publishes Restatements of the Law, model
statutes, and principles of law that are enormously influential
in the courts and legislatures, as well as in legal scholarship and
education.

In May 1992, the ALI rewrote the Prudent Investor Rule.
Here is some of what the Institute had to say in doing so
(emphasis mine):

- Investing in index funds that track major stock exchanges
  or widely published listings of publicly traded stocks is
  illustrative of a thoroughly passive but practical investment
  alternative to be considered by trustees seeking to include
  corporate equity in their portfolios.

- A trustee may find it preferable, for example, to reduce
  risk by mixing a moderately risky portfolio with essentially
  riskless assets (such as short-term federal obligations), rather
  than by developing a low-risk portfolio for the entire trust
  estate.

- *Active strategies, however, entail investigation and analysis
  expenses that increase general transaction costs, including capital
  gains taxation.* Accordingly, a decision to proceed with such
  a program involves judgments by the trustee that: a) gains
  from the course of action in question can reasonably be
  expected to *compensate for its additional costs and risks* b) the
  course of action to be *undertaken is reasonable in terms of its
  economic rationale and its role within the trust portfolio* c) there
  is a credible basis for concluding that the trustee—or the
  manager of a particular activity—possesses or has access to
  the competence necessary to carry out the program and,
  when delegation is involved, that its terms and supervision
  are appropriate.

By rewriting the Prudent Investor Rule, the ALI recognized both the significance and efficacy of MPT and that active management delivers inconsistent and poor results. The ALI had the following to say about market efficiency. In summary:

- Economic evidence shows that the major capital markets of this country are *highly efficient* in the sense that available information is rapidly digested and reflected in market prices.
- Fiduciaries and other investors are confronted with potent evidence that the application of expertise, investigation, and diligence in efforts to "beat the market" ordinarily promises little or no payoff, or even a negative payoff after taking account of research and transaction costs.
- Empirical research supporting the theory of efficient markets reveals that in such markets skilled professionals rarely have been able to identify underpriced securities with any regularity.
- Evidence shows that there is little correlation between fund managers' earlier successes and their ability to produce above-market returns in subsequent periods.

The Uniform Prudent Investor Act

The Uniform Prudent Investor Act (UPIA), adopted in 1994, reflects MPT and a total-return approach to the exercise of fiduciary investment discretion. The UPIA is currently the law in the vast majority of states and sets forth standards that govern the investment activities of trustees. It adopts MPT as the standard by which fiduciaries invest funds. The act does note that trustees have the authority to delegate their responsibilities as a prudent investor would. Thus, trustees/investors who do not have the knowledge, skill, time, or interest to prudently manage a portfolio should delegate that responsibility to an adviser who does. However, prudence in delegating the responsibilities must be observed. Section 9 (a) of the act states:

> The trustee shall exercise reasonable care, skill, and caution in (1) selecting an agent, (2) establishing the scope and terms of the delegation, consistent with the purposes and terms of the trust and (3) periodically reviewing the agent's actions in order to monitor the agent's performance and compliance with the terms of the delegation.

For those with fiduciary responsibility, adopting MPT makes sense because;

- It can provide the maximum expected return for a given level of risk.
- It provides relief from liability for fiduciaries who are not in the investment business by appointing competent managers or advisers who invest according to its tenets.

Faced with this restatement and recent legislative changes, trustees began a major switch from active to passive portfolio strategies. As recently as 25 years ago, very little was invested in passive funds. By June 30, 2009, the amount invested was about $4.8 trillion.[2]

The shift has occurred not only because of the overwhelming evidence, but also because pension fund managers must now ask themselves: "Do I want to invest in a way that has been recognized as prudent by the ALI? Or would I rather try to beat the market through an active management strategy, knowing that if I fail I may be forced to justify why I took such a strategy in the face of the academic evidence?"

The trend to passive investing is not only apparent in the institutional market, but is also rapidly gaining momentum in the retail market. Vanguard launched an S&P 500 Index fund with $11.4 million in assets in 1976. It took six years to cross the $100 million mark, but only four more to approach

$500 million in assets. In early 1997, it crossed $30 billion. As of August 2010, the fund had approximately $86.8 billion under management, and the Vanguard Total Stock Market Fund had over $126.4 billion under management. Both had long ago surpassed the actively managed Fidelity Magellan to become the largest retail funds in the world.

Even the bear market of 2008 through March 2009 did not stop the trend. Investors continued to add over $250 billion in assets in passive investment strategies from the end of 2007 through August 2009 and withdrew over $70 billion from actively managed funds. In the first half of 2009, almost $22 billion of new cash was added to equity index funds, while $20 billion was withdrawn from active stock funds.[3] The result will be that a lot more of the returns the market provides will end up in the accounts of investors instead of in the wallets of active managers.

While individual investors are waking up to the failure of active management, they lag institutional investors in the shift to passive investing. According to the Investment Company Institute, at year-end 2007 there was $1.5 trillion invested in index funds and exchange-traded funds (ETFs), representing just 12.5 percent of the total invested in mutual funds.[4] The explanation for the smaller share among individual investors is that institutional investors are more aware of the academic research.

The good news is that the Investment Company Institute's 2010 annual report showed that index funds and ETFs (almost all of which are passively managed) continued to gain market share. For example, at the end of 2009, index mutual funds had increased their market share to 13.7 percent. It is worth noting that the figures for 2000 and 1995 were just 9 percent and 4 percent, respectively.[5] While active managers will probably never go the way of buggy-whip manufacturers, their market share seems sure to continue to decline as investors continue to abandon the quest for alpha and accept market returns.

Despite all the evidence, despite the UPIA, and despite the ALI's Third Restatement of Trusts, Wall Street and most of the financial media continue to tout the benefits of active investing. The question is: Why? Simply, it is a matter of having their own interests at heart, not yours. That is the subject of Chapter 9.

Chapter 9

Whose Interests Do They Have at Heart?

An out-of-town visitor was being shown the wonders of the New York financial district. When the party arrived at the Battery, one of his guides indicated some handsome ships riding at anchor. He said, "Look, those are the bankers' and brokers' yachts." The naïve customer asked: "Where are the customers' yachts?"[1]

Wall Street needs and wants you to play the game of active investing. They know that your odds of outperforming appropriate benchmarks are so low, it is not in your interest to play. They need you to play so *they* (not you) make the most money. They make it by charging high fees for active management that persistently delivers poor performance. The financial media also want and need you to play so you "tune in." They need you to become hooked on investment noise (or what author Jane Bryant Quinn called *investment porn*), as that is what produces profits for them. Their interests are not aligned with the interest of investors.

Advice from Professional Investors

Gary Gensler is the chairman of the U.S. Commodity Futures Trading Commission. From 1999 through 2001, he was Undersecretary of Domestic Finance at the Department of the Treasury. From 1997 through 2001 he was Assistant Secretary of Financial Markets. Gensler also spent 18 years at Goldman Sachs, rising to cohead of finance. After leaving the Treasury, he acted as a senior adviser to Senator Paul Sarbanes, one of the authors of legislation that eventually became the Sarbanes-Oxley Act, designed to bring greater oversight to the accounting industry and reform of corporate governance. Along with co-author Gregory Arthur Baer, a former assistant secretary for financial institutions at the U.S. Department of the Treasury, he wrote *The Great Mutual Fund Trap*. Gensler and Baer warned investors:

> The mutual fund and brokerage industries belittle indexing because it is deadly competition for their higher margin products. The financial media ignore it because it makes such lousy copy.[2]

They added:

> With all that is known about the poor results of active stock picking, why do so many investors still buy high-cost mutual funds and churn their stock portfolios? One major reason is because they are told to do so, every day, explicitly or implicitly, by the financial media and Wall Street.[3]

Admissions from Industry Practitioners and Academics

Dan Ariely is a professor of behavioral economics at Duke University and a visiting professor at MIT's Media Laboratory. He is also the author of *Predictably Irrational.* Quoting Pulitzer Prize–winning author and political activist Upton Sinclair, he states, "It is difficult to get a man to understand something when his salary depends on his not understanding it."[4]

Ariely recognized that when there is a conflict of interest, it is hard for those whose incomes depend on exploiting that conflict to admit the problem. Despite the difficulty, the following provides evidence of the conflicts facing Wall Street and the financial media.

We begin with an internal memo from a major brokerage firm. It would be hard to find more damning evidence.

> Index funds are passively managed mutual funds. They simply buy and hold all the stocks of a particular market index such as the S&P 500. . . . Because their turnover is low and they don't require large research staffs, most have low operating expenses. . . . The returns of an index fund are a function of two factors: the performance of the index itself, and the fees to operate and distribute the mutual fund. For a fund to be successful in the brokerage community it must adequately compensate brokers either through an up-front commission or an ongoing service fee or both. As a result, a broker-sold index fund would underperform not only the index but also a no-load index mutual fund. These are reasons why most index funds are offered by no-load fund groups.

Brokers do not sell index funds because they do not perform well. They are not sold because investors can buy them cheaper elsewhere. Mutual fund sponsors avoid indexing because, while the record makes clear it is the winning strategy for *investors,* it is not very profitable for fund sponsors. They see indexing as the losing *business* strategy.

For these reasons, Wall Street does not educate consumers about the virtues of passive management and continues to extol the dubious virtues of active management. It is clearly in the interest of Wall Street to charge you 1.5 percent for underperforming actively managed funds rather than about 0.1 percent to 0.5 percent for index funds.

The following tale is further evidence of the problem of conflicting interests.

CIBC is one of Canada's largest banks. In the mid-1990s, it made the decision to focus on growing its wealth management business. The problem was that the family of CIBC mutual funds had delivered poor results, leaving them with a marketing dilemma. The bank decided that the solution to their problem was to tout index funds as the winning strategy for investors. The bank created a family of index funds and placed Ted Cadsby in charge. His mission was to spread the gospel of the benefits of passive investing. He became a very public spokesman for the bank. Cadsby authored *The Power of Index Funds*, in which he railed against the evils of active management.

Cadsby was successful in his mission—assets under management doubled to $24 billion in just four years. CIBC had the second-fastest growing fund family among Canadian banks. Then Cadsby disappeared from public view. According to the *Financial Post*, Cadsby had been told to "quiet down." Why? Because the winning strategy for investors was the losing strategy for the bank!

The bank had recently purchased Merrill Lynch Canada's retail brokerage arm (including $4.5 billion in actively managed mutual fund assets), as well as TAL Global Asset Management Inc., which managed over $50 billion in assets, including $4 billion in retail mutual funds (under the Talvest name). These funds charged the kind of outrageously high fees against which Cadsby had been railing. The typical Talvest fund charged about 2.5 percent per annum. Some of its global funds charged over 3 percent per annum. Merrill's fund fees were similar.[5]

Ted Lux was a stockbroker at Morgan Stanley Dean Witter. After leaving, he wrote *Exposing the Wheel Spin on Wall Street*. He warned about the conflicts of interest between Wall Street and its clients:

> While I was at Morgan Stanley Dean Witter I never once came across a broker talking to a client about the problems turnover creates with mutual fund investing. Nor capital gains tax. Nor the effect the tax has on lowering the investor's true rate of return. Simply put, the idea or notion of after-tax returns was shoved aside and under the rug.[6]

Just as it is not in the interests of Wall Street for investors to give up the quest for the Holy Grail of alpha, neither is it in the interests of the financial media. Consider the following two admissions. The August 1995 edition of *Money* stated: "Bogle [of the Vanguard group of funds, the largest provider of retail index funds] wins: Index funds should be the core of most portfolios today."

The *Wall Street Journal* joined in the chorus of warnings against actively managed funds: "A decade of results throws cold water on the notion that strategists exhibit any special ability to time the markets."[7]

The irony in these statements is that none of the publications will give indexing a wholehearted endorsement. If readers believed in indexing, who would buy publications touting which stocks and mutual funds to buy? The primary objective of most financial publications is not to make their readers wealthy. Instead, it is to get readers to buy more of what they are selling—their magazines. In addition, these magazines carry a large amount of advertising from actively managed mutual funds. The publishers do not want to risk losing valuable advertising revenue.

Even *BusinessWeek* has warned investors about the conflict of interest between Wall Street and its clients: "It has been a problem since the dawn of the retail brokerage business. Brokers have a strong incentive to get customers to trade when it might be in clients' interests to do nothing."[8]

John Merrill, author of *Outperforming the Market*, warned investors to be aware of the bias of the financial press:

> First and foremost, the financial media is no different than other media. Job number one is to maintain and increase readers and viewers. This forces their primary focus to be on today. It is in their interest to hook their audience on daily information (or weekly or monthly, depending on publishing or broadcasting dates). It is a huge challenge—to make each day's market activity seem meaningful.[9]

Jean Baptiste Colbert, finance minister to Louis XIV, described the act of generating revenue in this colorful way: "The art of taxation consists in so plucking the goose as to procure the greatest quantity of feathers with the least possible amount of hissing."[10]

The same can be said of active managers: They want to keep plucking those large management fees from the pockets of individual investors with the least possible amount of hissing. In order to continue doing so, they must keep alive the myth that active management works.

Frank Knight, a professor of economics at the University of Chicago from 1928 until his death in 1972 at the age of 87, said it best when he claimed that economic theory was not at all obscure or complicated, but that most people had a vested interest in refusing to recognize what was "insultingly obvious."[11]

The financial media also have conflicts. Consider this admission from Steve Forbes, publisher of the magazine that bears his name: "You make more money selling advice than following it. It's one of the things we count on in the magazine business—along with the short memory of our readers."[12]

And consider this from an anonymous writer for *Fortune*: "By day we write 'Six Funds to Buy NOW!' We seem to delight in dangerous sectors like technology. We appear fascinated with one-week returns. By night, however, we invest in sensible index funds. Unfortunately, rational, pro-index fund stories don't sell magazines, cause hits on Web sites, or boost Nielsen ratings."[13]

Caroline Baum is the author of *Just What I Said* and a columnist for *Bloomberg. Bloomberg* is in the business of selling the noise. Yet Baum, writing for *Bloomberg,* stated: "Pundits can't predict the future to save their lives, but when it comes to explaining the past, nobody does it better."[14]

Scott Burns has been a personal financial columnist for over 40 years. Writing for the *Dallas Morning News*, Burns warned investors:

> Index strategies work, not because of market timing, but because not making investment decisions works better than making investment decisions. No one on Wall Street wants to hear this because they make their livings by making investment decisions and charging us for it. The end result of Wall Street investment decisions is great for them (commissions, management fees, free trips, expense-paid bachelor parties, etc.). But the people who put up the money—you and me—rarely benefit. There are several reasons for this. First, it costs a lot of money to have someone make investment decisions. Wall Street has been charging all the traffic will bear for decades. Second, it costs money to execute those decisions—in commissions and market maker spreads.
>
> How this continues, year after year, is beyond me. If a group of surgeons learned (however reluctantly) that a procedure harmed their patients about 70 percent of the time, they would be duty-bound to stop performing the procedure. Wall Street just keeps doing its "procedure," regardless of efficacy, because it makes their Mercedes payment.[15]

If you are not yet convinced about whose interests Wall Street has at heart, I have saved the best for last. The following quotation was provided to me by attorney Dan Solin, author of *Does Your Broker Owe You Money?*

The source is an unnamed former vice president of sales of a major broker-dealer. The source is unnamed because arbitration cases prevent disclosure. Solin had represented an ex-broker who worked for two major firms. The ex-broker testified to almost precisely this speech being given to him. Dan added that he has reviewed tens of thousands of pages of internal broker-dealer documents. From his perspective, the following accurately reflects the prevailing views of management in the brokerage industry:

> My branch managers only want producers who will pick the gold from their grandmother's teeth. Now that we have the gun to your head and we are into your pockets, do as you are told, sell what we want you to sell when we want you to sell it, or we'll fire you and hire someone else. Then we will sue you for what we lent you and make damn well sure that you never see your book of business again.

A Triumph of Hope over Experience

Steve Galbraith teaches security analysis at Columbia University in its MBA program. He was the former chief U.S. investment strategist at Morgan Stanley. He also co-authored Morgan Stanley's *US Investment Perspectives*. In March 2002, Galbraith invited John Bogle, the founder and former chairman of the Vanguard Group and a strong advocate of passive investing, to speak to his class.

In a letter to investors in the April 3, 2002, issue, Galbraith related the following about Bogle's presentation:

> He laid out the case against active management and for indexing quite powerfully. My guess is that more than a few students left the class wondering just what the heck their hard-earned tuition dollars were doing going to a class devoted to the seemingly impossible— analyzing securities to achieve better-than-market returns. . . . At least the students have the excuse of being early in their careers; what's mine for staying the course in my current role?

He also admitted: "*We recognize that the odds are against active managers.*" [Emphasis mine]

Galbraith pointed out that actual returns to investors in the greatest bull market ever ranged "from the subprime to the ridiculous." Galbraith closed his letter on a very revealing note: "From our perspective, *perhaps in a triumph of hope over experience*, we continue to believe active managers can add value." [Emphasis mine] Given the role of his employer, to believe otherwise would be committing professional suicide. The winning strategy for investors is simply to accept market returns. However, that is not the winning strategy for Morgan Stanley.

You don't have to play the game of active management. Instead, you can earn market (not average) rates of return with low expenses and high tax efficiency. You can do so by investing in passively managed investment vehicles, virtually guaranteeing that you will outperform the majority of both professionals and individual investors. Let's see why this must be so.

The Arithmetic of Active Management

William Sharpe is a professor of finance, emeritus, at Stanford University's Graduate School of Business and the winner of the 1990 Nobel Memorial Prize in economic science. Along with co-winners Harry Markowitz and Merton Miller, Sharpe was awarded the prize for pioneering work on the theory of financial economics. He has also served as president of the American Finance Association.

In 1991, Sharpe wrote his now famous paper, *The Arithmetic of Active Management*, in which he demonstrated that oft-heard claims such as "This is a stock picker's year when active managers will beat their respective indices," "In small caps and emerging markets especially you're better off with active managers," and "Active managers can protect you from bear markets" can be made only by "assuming that the laws of arithmetic have been suspended for the convenience of those who choose to pursue careers as active managers."[16]

Sharpe explained it this way:

> If "active" and "passive" management styles are defined in sensible ways, it must be the case that:
>
> (1) before costs, the return on the average actively managed dollar will equal the return on the average passively managed dollar and
> (2) after costs, the return on the average actively managed dollar will be less than the return on the average passively managed dollar.
>
> These assertions will hold for *any* time period. Moreover, they depend *only* on the laws of addition, subtraction, multiplication and division. Nothing else is required. To repeat: Properly measured, the average actively managed dollar must underperform the average passively managed dollar, net of costs. Empirical analyses that appear to refute this principle are guilty of improper measurement.[17]

A simple example will demonstrate conclusively that active investing must, in aggregate, be a loser's game, despite claims to the contrary. The market is made up of only two types of investors: active and passive.

Assume that 70 percent of investors are active and 30 percent of investors are passive. (The outcome is the same regardless of the percentages used.) Assume the market returns 10 percent. On a pre-expense basis, investors in the Vanguard Total Stock Market Fund must earn 10 percent. What rate of return, before expenses, must the active managers have earned? Because the sum of the parts must equal the whole, collectively, active managers must also have earned 10 percent. The following equations show the math:

A = Total Stock Market, B = Active Investors,
C = Passive Investors

A = B + C

X = Rate of return earned by active investors

10% (100%) = X% (70%) + 10% (30%)

X must equal 10%

Note that if you change the percentages of market share, the outcome is exactly the same. Thus, even if index funds take over 90 percent of the market, the results will be the same.

Because all stocks must be owned by someone, if one active investor outperforms because he overweighted the top-performing stocks, another active investor must have underperformed by underweighting those very same stocks. The investor who outperformed had to buy those winning securities from someone. Since passive investors simply buy and hold, the stock must have been sold by another active investor. In aggregate, on a pre-expense basis, active investors earn the same market rate of return as do passive investors.

The Math Is Always the Same

If, instead of using the total stock market, we substituted the S&P 500 Index, small-cap stocks, value stocks, real estate, emerging markets, or any other asset class, we would come to exactly the same conclusion. That exposes the lie that active management works in "inefficient" asset classes like small-cap and emerging market stocks.

The same thing is true for bull and bear markets. If the market loses 10 percent, the Vanguard Total Stock Market Fund will also lose 10 percent on a pre-expense basis—in aggregate, so must active investors. The math doesn't change if the bull is rampaging or the bear comes out of hibernation—in aggregate, active management must earn the same pre-expense gross return as passive management, regardless of asset class or market condition.

The Costs of Active Investing

So far, we have been discussing gross returns. Investors don't earn gross returns; they earn returns net of expenses. To get to the net returns, we must subtract all costs, including trading costs. The most obvious cost is a fund's expense ratio. While the typical actively managed fund has an expense ratio of about 1.5 percent, the expense ratio of most index funds ranges from just 0.1 to 0.5 percent. Mutual funds also incur trading costs that are related to turnover.

Trading Costs

Trading costs are not limited to just commissions, but also include the difference between the bid and offer. When buying or selling large amounts of stock, funds can incur market impact costs.

An estimate of the negative impact of the trading (turnover) of active managers is provided by a Morningstar study. Morningstar divided mutual funds into two categories: those with an average holding period greater than five years (less than 20 percent turnover) and those with an average holding period of less than one year (turnover greater than 100 percent). Over a 10-year period, Morningstar found that low-turnover funds returned an average of 12.87 percent per annum. On average, high-turnover funds gained only 11.29 percent per annum. Relative to low-turnover funds, trading costs (and perhaps higher operating expenses) reduced returns of the high-turnover funds by 1.58 percent per annum.[18]

Taxes

For taxable accounts, taxes are often the greatest expense of active management. The negative impact of the burden of taxes is a result of fund distributions. The incremental tax cost of active versus passive funds can easily exceed 1 percent per annum. For example, John Bogle studied the effect of taxes on returns and found:

- For the 15-year period ending June 30, 1998, the Vanguard 500 Index Fund provided pretax returns of 16.9 percent per annum.
- The fund lost 1.9 percent per annum to taxes. Its after-tax return of 15 percent per annum meant that the fund's tax efficiency was 89 percent.
- The average actively managed fund provided pretax returns of 13.6 percent and after-tax returns of just 10.8 percent.
- The fund lost 2.8 percent per annum to taxes, a tax efficiency of just 79 percent.[19]

How great a hurdle is the burden of taxes? Consider the following:

Ted Aronson is the founder of Aronson + partners (now Aronson+Johnson+Ortiz), an institutional money manager with about $18 billion in assets under management. In an interview with *Barron's*, he admitted:[20]

- "I never forget that the devil sitting on my shoulder [is] low-cost passive funds. They win because they lose less."

- "That's why none of my 20 clients are taxable. Because, once you introduce taxes—and it doesn't matter whether it's a 12- or 18-month holding period—*active management probably has an insurmountable hurdle.* We have been asked to run taxable money—and declined. The costs of our active strategies are high enough without paying Uncle Sam." [Emphasis mine]
- "Capital gains taxes, when combined with transactions costs and fees, make indexing profoundly advantaged, I'm sorry to say."
- "All of the partners are in the same situation—our retirement dough is here. But not our taxable investments."
- "If you crunch the numbers turnover has to come down, not to low, but to super-low, like 15–20 percent, or taxes kill you. That's the real dirty little secret in our business: Because mutual funds are bought and sold with virtually no attention attached to tax efficiency."
- "My wife, three children and I have taxable money in eight of the Vanguard index funds."

There is one other cost of active management.

The Cost of Cash

It is often overlooked because it is hidden. It is the "cost of cash." The cost of cash is a result of a mutual fund's holding cash instead of being fully invested in the market. Since, over the long term, stocks have provided a higher return than cash (or the equivalent of one-month Treasury bills), holding cash in an effort to time the market reduces returns. A study by Russ Wermers found that nonequity holdings reduced returns for the average actively managed equity fund by 0.7 percent.[21]

In each of the preceding cases, because of operating expenses, trading costs, taxes, and the cost of cash, the cost of implementing a passive strategy will be less than that of an active one. Thus, in aggregate, passive investors must earn higher net returns than active investors. As Sharpe pointed out, the mathematical facts cannot be denied. The bottom line is that active management is, in aggregate, a negative-sum game.

An Expensive Quest

How much is the quest for the Holy Grail of alpha costing investors? Professor Ken French sought the answer to that in his 2008 study "The Cost of Active Investing."[22] The study covered the period 1980–2006 and included mutual funds, exchange-traded funds (ETFs), hedge funds, and institutional funds. French compared the total costs of active management (fees, expenses, and trading costs) with an estimate of costs if everyone invested passively—the difference being the cost of active management. The following is a summary of his findings:

- The value-weighted cost of all (active and passive) equity mutual funds fell from 2.08 percent of assets under management in 1980 to 0.95 percent in 2006.
- Institutional costs are dramatically lower. The value-weighted costs for institutions fell from 0.34 percent in 1980 to 0.23 percent in 2006. Institutional costs declined for two reasons. First, the costs they pay for active and passive investments declined. Second, institutions shifted a large portion of their U.S. equity holdings from active to passive.
- The average annual hedge fund fee (expense ratio plus performance fee) for 1996 to 2007 was 4.26 percent of assets. Because they pay two layers of fees, the average for investors who buy through funds of hedge funds was much higher—6.52 percent.

French estimated that in 2006 the total cost of investing, the fees and expenses paid for mutual funds, the investment management costs paid by institutions, the fees paid to hedge funds and funds of funds, and the transaction costs paid by all traders was 0.75 percent of the value of all New York Stock Exchange, American Stock Exchange, and Nasdaq stocks. He also estimated that if all investors paid passive fees, and there were no hedge funds, the cost of investing in 2006 would have been just 0.09 percent. The difference between the actual and passive estimates measures the cost of active investing. Bottom line: active investors are engaging in a massive transfer of wealth—about $80 billion annually (based on market capitalization of about $12 trillion)—from their own wallets to those of the purveyors of actively managed products and market makers.

Michael Jensen is a professor emeritus at Harvard University and a major contributor to modern financial theory, having published over 100 scientific papers. Here is what he had to say on the subject of the costs of active investing: "It is difficult to systematically beat the market. But it is not difficult to systematically throw money down a rat hole by generating commissions (and other costs)."[23]

Despite the enormity of the costs of active investing, French's estimate is too low. The reason is that it does not take into account the incremental burden of higher taxes incurred by active investors with taxable holdings. As *Wall Street Journal* personal financial columnist Jonathan Clements noted: "If index funds look great before taxes, their performance is almost unbeatable after taxes, thanks to their low turnover and thus slow realization of capital gains."[24]

French made the important observation that the cost of active investing is not a pure loss to society—the price discovery activities of active managers improve the accuracy of financial prices and allow for an efficient allocation of capital.

The good news for passive investors is they get to be "free riders," benefiting from the activities of active managers without paying the costs.

Summary

The evidence presented demonstrates that, in aggregate, active management is a negative-sum game, also known as a loser's game. That does not mean that all active investors produce below benchmark returns. Active management does hold out the hope of outperformance. However, it is probably safe to say that there is no other effort on which such an expense is incurred every year with such poor results.

Hopefully, all of the evidence presented has convinced you that the quest for the Holy Grail of alpha is the triumph of hope, hype, and marketing over wisdom and experience. If you still doubt this conclusion, consider the following quotations from two legendary investors. On the supposed advantages of investment professionals, Peter Lynch opined: "[Investors] think of the so-called professionals, with all their computers and all their power, as having all the advantages. That is total crap. . . . They'd be better off in an index fund."[25]

The following three quotations are from Warren Buffett:

> Most investors, both institutional and individual, will find that the best way to own common stocks is through an index fund that charges minimal fees. Those following this path are sure to beat the net results (after fees and expenses) delivered by the great majority of investment professionals.[26]

In an interview with *Fortune*, Buffett offered this advice: "Buying an index fund over a long period of time makes the most sense."[27]

Buffett also offered this observation in his 2004 Annual Letter to shareholders of Berkshire Hathaway:

> Over the 35 years, American business has delivered terrific results. It should therefore have been easy for investors to earn juicy returns: All they had to do was piggyback Corporate America in a diversified, low-expense way. An index fund that they never touched would have done the job. Instead many investors have had experiences ranging from mediocre to disastrous.

And, finally, in case you are not yet convinced that Wall Street does not have your interests at heart, consider this from ex-Salomon Brothers employee and author Michael Lewis:

> A vast industry of stockbrokers, financial planners, and investment advisers skims a fortune for themselves off the top in exchange for passing their clients' money on to people who, as a group, cannot possibly outperform the market.[28]

A fitting close to this chapter is the following tale. John, a stockbroker, has just died. An angel greets him at the pearly gates.

Angel: John, I have good news and bad news for you. Which would you prefer first?

John: Might as well get the bad news out of the way.

Angel: You have not done enough good things to get into heaven.

John: Oh, my goodness. What could possibly be the good news?

Angel: You did not do enough bad things to go to that other place.

John: What happens to me now?

Angel: Actually, we give you a choice. We let you visit both places, and you get to decide where you want to spend eternity. The only caveat is that once the choice is made, it is irrevocable. Where would you like to go first?

John: Let's try heaven first.

The angel snaps his fingers and John is in heaven—a beautiful, pastoral setting with angels flying around; people playing musical instruments; others reading books; or whatever you might imagine heaven to be. Upon his return, the angel asks:

Angel: So what do you think?

John: It's just like I imagined it. But, as long as I have a choice, I might as well visit the other place.

The angel snaps his fingers once again, and John finds himself surrounded by beautiful women, swimming pools, golf courses, theatres, casinos, and so on. Upon his return, the angel again asks what he thinks.

John: Heaven was awfully nice, but I think the other place is more me. I have decided to go there.

Angel: Are you sure? Because the choice is irrevocable.

John: I am sure.

The angel snaps his fingers, and John arrives in hell. It is 120 degrees, and everyone is wearing heavy chains and pounding on rocks with a sledgehammer. The devil greets him.

John: What is this?

Devil: Yesterday, you were a prospect. Today, you're my client.

Chapter 10

How to Play the Winner's Game

As we discussed in Chapter 2, if anyone should be able to beat the market, it should be the pension plans of large companies. They have all the advantages over individual investors, including paying significantly lower fees and not having the burden of taxes to overcome. Yet we saw the evidence that pension plans have had a difficult time outperforming appropriate benchmarks. The following is another example of their inability to beat simple indexing strategies.

FutureMetrics is a consulting firm that maintains an extensive database on corporate defined benefit plans. They studied the performance of 192 major U.S. corporate pension plans for the 18-year period 1988–2005.[1] Since it is estimated that the average pension plan has an allocation of 60 percent equities and 40 percent fixed income, we can compare the realized returns of these plans to a benchmark portfolio with an asset allocation of 60 percent S&P 500 Index and 40 percent Barclays Capital Intermediate Government/Corporate Bond Index (range, 1–10 years). This passive portfolio could have been implemented by each of the plans as an alternative to active strategies. Less than 30 percent of the pension plans outperformed the simple indexing strategy.

Based on my experience, it is safe to say that the poor results could not be attributed to poor governance. Certainly, the investment policy committee members of the pension plans considered themselves good stewards. In other words, they were smart people who performed their roles diligently—yet they still failed. With such a high percentage failing, it is unlikely they failed because of bad luck. If it was not bad luck, and it was not failure of process, what led to such a high failure rate? The answer is the strategy they used: active management was a losing strategy.

The story is actually worse than even these dismal results suggest. Consider that a large number of these pension plans invested at least some small portion of their plans in riskier asset classes such as small-cap and value stocks, high-yield bonds, venture capital, and emerging-market equities. As higher-risk asset classes, they have higher expected returns. Yet despite this advantage, for the time period surveyed, over 70 percent of the funds failed to beat "par." These pension plans were likely taking more risk, and yet they earned lower, not higher, returns.

Consider also that since the average pension plan has an allocation of 60 percent equities and 40 percent bonds, some surely have a higher equity allocation. Given that equities outperformed bonds over the period of the study, any plan with an allocation of more than 60 percent stocks would have had an advantage. Again, these plans were taking more risk but were "rewarded" with lower returns.

Ask yourself what advantage you have that would allow you to have a high degree of confidence that you would be likely to succeed where the plans with the advantages of lower costs failed with such great frequency? I have yet to meet an individual or investment committee that could provide an answer.

Indexing Is More than the S&P 500 Index

Writing for the *Wall Street Journal*, Jonathan Clements noted: "Indexing is a wonderful strategy. It's a shame most folks do it wrong."[2] He was referring to his belief that most investors who use index funds limit themselves to funds that mimic the S&P 500. In this chapter, you will see how expanding on a simple S&P 500 indexing strategy can improve results. It will also show you how to outperform the vast majority of institutional investors.

The power of Modern Portfolio Theory (MPT) will be demonstrated by following the performance of a "control" portfolio, with a traditional asset allocation of 60 percent equities and 40 percent fixed income over the 35-year period 1975–2009. This period was chosen because it is the longest for which we have data on the indices used. Again, this 60/40 allocation is typical of the asset allocation of U.S. pension plans, so-called balanced mutual funds and many individual investors. While maintaining the same 60 percent stock/40 percent bond allocation, we will expand our investment universe to other equity asset classes.

We will begin with the same two investments that served as the benchmark in the FutureMetrics example, the S&P 500 Index for the equity allocation and the Barclays Capital Intermediate Government/Credit Bond Index for the fixed income allocation.

First, we will see how the portfolio performed if an investor had the patience to stay with this allocation from 1975 through 2009 and rebalanced annually. We then demonstrate how the portfolio's performance could have been made more efficient by increasing its diversification across asset classes. We do so in five steps.

Portfolio 1

S&P 500 Index   60%
Barclays Capital Intermediate Government/
   Credit Bond Index   40%

1975–2009

Annualized Return (%)	Annual Standard Deviation (%)
10.6	11.3

Sources: S&P, Barclays

By changing the composition of the control portfolio through a step-by-step process, we will see how we can improve the efficiency of our portfolio. To avoid being accused of data mining, we will alter our allocations by arbitrarily "cutting things in half."

Step 1: The most important diversification on the equity side is to add an exposure to international equities. Therefore, we reduce our allocation to the S&P 500 from 60 percent to 30 percent and allocate 30 percent to the MSCI EAFE (Europe, Australasia, and the Far East) Index.

Portfolio 2

S&P 500 Index   30%
MSCI EAFE Index   30%
Barclays Capital Intermediate Government/
   Credit Bond Index   40%

1975–2009

	Annualized Return (%)	Annual Standard Deviation (%)
Portfolio 1	10.6	11.3
Portfolio 2	10.6	11.3

Sources: S&P, MSCI Inc., Barclays

Step 2: Our next step is to diversify our domestic equity holdings to include small caps. We shift half our 30 percent allocation to the S&P 500 Index to a small-cap index.

Portfolio 3

S&P 500 Index	15%
Fama/French US Small Cap Index	15%
MSCI EAFE Index	30%
Barclays Capital Intermediate Government/ Credit Bond Index	40%

1975–2009

	Annualized Return (%)	Annual Standard Deviation (%)
Portfolio 1	10.6	11.3
Portfolio 2	10.6	11.3
Portfolio 3	11.2	11.5

Sources: S&P, MSCI Inc., Barclays, CRSP®

Step 3: Our next step is to shift half our 15 percent allocations to domestic large and small caps to domestic large value and small value.

Portfolio 4

S&P 500 Index	7.5%
Fama/French US Large Value Index (ex utilities)	7.5%
Fama/French US Small Cap Index	7.5%
Fama/French US Small Value Index (ex utilities)	7.5%
MSCI EAFE Index	30%
Barclays Capital Intermediate Government/ Credit Bond Index	40%

1975–2009

	Annualized Return (%)	Annual Standard Deviation (%)
Portfolio 1	10.6	11.3
Portfolio 2	10.6	11.3
Portfolio 3	11.2	11.5
Portfolio 4	11.5	11.8

Sources: S&P, MSCI Inc., Barclays, CRSP®

Step 4: Our next step is to diversify our international equity holdings to include value stocks. (I would have included small-cap stocks here, but the MSCI EAFE Small Cap Index data only goes back to 1999.) We shift half our 30 percent allocation to the MSCI EAFE to the MSCI EAFE Value Index.

Portfolio 5

S&P 500 Index	7.5%
Fama/French US Large Value Index (ex utilities)	7.5%
Fama/French US Small Cap Index	7.5%
Fama/French US Small Value Index (ex utilities)	7.5%
MSCI EAFE Index	15%
MSCI EAFE Value Index	15%
Barclays Capital Intermediate Government/ Credit Bond Index	40%

1975–2009

	Annualized Return (%)	Annual Standard Deviation (%)
Portfolio 1	10.6	11.3
Portfolio 2	10.6	11.3

Portfolio 3	11.2	11.5
Portfolio 4	11.5	11.8
Portfolio 5	11.8	11.9

Sources: S&P, MSCI Inc., Barclays, CRSP®

The effect of our changes has been to increase the return on the portfolio from 10.6 percent to 11.8 percent (1.2 percent), while increasing the portfolio's volatility from 11.3 to 11.9 percent (just 0.6 percent). In relative terms, we increased the return by about 11 percent, while volatility increased about 5 percent. The result is a more efficient portfolio.

We have one more step to consider. Commodities diversify some of the risks of investing in stocks. They also diversify the risks of investing in bonds. We add a 4 percent allocation to the Goldman Sachs Commodity Index (S&P/GSCI), reducing each of our four domestic equity allocations by 0.5 percent (from 7.5 to 7.0) and both the international equity allocations by 1 percent (from 15 to 14).

Portfolio 6

S&P 500 Index	7%
Fama/French US Large Value Index (ex utilities)	7%
Fama/French US Small Cap Index	7%
Fama/French US Small Value Index (ex utilities)	7%
MSCI EAFE Index	14%
MSCI EAFE Value Index	14%
S&P/GSCI	4%
Barclays Capital Intermediate Government/ Credit Bond Index	40%

1975–2009

	Annualized Return (%)	Annual Standard Deviation (%)
Portfolio 1	10.6	11.3
Portfolio 2	10.6	11.3
Portfolio 3	11.2	11.5
Portfolio 4	11.5	11.8
Portfolio 5	11.8	11.9
Portfolio 6	11.6	11.2

Sources: S&P, MSCI Inc., Barclays, CRSP®

The net result of all of our changes is that we now have a portfolio that produced both higher returns with less volatility, clearly a more efficient portfolio. On an absolute basis, returns increased 1.0 percent (from 10.6 to 11.6), and volatility fell by 0.1 percent (from 11.3 to 11.2). On a relative basis, returns increased by about 9 percent, and volatility fell by about 1 percent.

Does Passive Investing Produce Average Returns?

Through the step-by-step process described above, it becomes clear that one of the major criticisms of passive portfolio management—it produces *average* returns—is false. There was nothing "average" about the returns of any of the six portfolios we explored. Certainly, the returns were greater than those of the average investor with a similar equity allocation, be it individual or institutional. Remember that about 70 percent of the pension plans could not even beat Portfolio 1.

Passive investing produces *market*, not average, returns— and it does so in a relatively low-cost and tax-efficient manner.

The average actively managed fund produces below-market results; it does so with great persistency and in a tax-inefficient manner.

By playing the winner's game of accepting market returns, investors will almost certainly outperform the vast majority of both individual and institutional investors who choose to play the active game. There is only one caveat. Investors must learn to act like a postage stamp. The lowly postage stamp does only one thing, but it does it exceedingly well—it sticks to its letter until it reaches its destination. Investors must stick to their investment plan (asset allocation) until they reach their financial goals. Their only activities should be rebalancing, tax-loss harvesting, and continuing to save and add to their portfolios.

Before concluding, we need to address one more critical part of playing the winner's game—the wisdom to know you have enough.

Enough

Author Kurt Vonnegut related this story about fellow author Joseph Heller. The two were at a billionaire's party on Shelter Island. Vonnegut asked Heller how it made him feel that the host may have made more money in one day than *Catch-22* (Heller's most famous work) did in its entire run. Heller replied that he had something the host could never have: "The knowledge that I've got enough."[3]

In 2009, I was asked to do an investment seminar for Tiger 21, a group of very high-net-worth individuals. One of the issues the group asked me to address was: how do the rich think about risk, and how should they think about it? What follows was my answer:

Unless one inherits their wealth, the most common way large fortunes are created is by taking lots of risk, often concentrating that risk in a personally owned business. Thus, high-net-worth individuals are typically successful entrepreneurs. By definition, they are risk takers who have known success. That provides them with confidence in their ability to take risk. That confidence often creates the willingness to take risks. In addition, given that they have large fortunes, they also have the ability to take risk. And that combination typically leads people to continue to take risks.

However, the ability and willingness to take risk are only two of the three criteria one should consider when deciding on an investment policy. The third and often overlooked criterion is the *need* to take risk. A great irony is that those who have the most ability and willingness to take risk have the least need to take it.

Those with sufficient wealth to meet all their needs should consider that the strategy to get rich is entirely different than the strategy to stay rich. The strategy to get rich is to take risks, typically in one's own business. But the strategy to stay rich is to minimize risk, diversify the risks you take, and avoid spending too much. I explained that since the objective of the Tiger 21 members was now to stay rich, it was important to create a new investment plan incorporating that goal.

When deciding on the appropriate asset allocation, investors should consider their *marginal utility of wealth*—how much any potential incremental wealth is worth relative to the risk that must be accepted to achieve a greater *expected* return. While more money is always better than less, at some point most people achieve a lifestyle with which they are comfortable. At that point, taking on incremental risk to achieve a higher net worth no longer makes sense: the potential damage of an unexpected negative outcome far exceeds the potential benefit gained from incremental wealth.

Each investor needs to decide at what level of wealth their unique utility of wealth curve starts flattening out and begins bending sharply to the right. Beyond this point, there is little reason to take incremental risk to achieve a higher *expected* return. Many wealthy investors have experienced devastating losses that could easily have been avoided if they had the wisdom to know what author Joseph Heller knew.

The lesson about knowing when enough is enough can be learned from the following story. In early 2003, I met with a married couple in their 70s with financial assets of $3 million. Three years earlier, their portfolio was worth $13 million. The only way they could have experienced that kind of loss was if they had held a portfolio that was almost all equities and heavily concentrated in U.S. large-cap growth stocks, especially technology stocks. They confirmed that my assumption was correct. They told me they had been working with a financial adviser during this period, demonstrating that while good advice does not have to be expensive, bad advice almost always costs you dearly.

I asked the couple if doubling their portfolio to $26 million would have led to any meaningful change in the quality of their lives? The response was a definite "no." I remarked that the experience of watching $13 million shrink to $3 million must have been very painful, and they probably had spent many sleepless nights. They agreed. I then asked why they took the risks they did, knowing the potential benefit was not going to change their lives very much but a negative outcome like the one they experienced would be so painful. The wife turned to the husband and punched him on the arm, exclaiming, "I told you so!"

This sad story demonstrates that some risks are not worth taking. Prudent investors don't take more risk than they have the ability, willingness, or *need* to take. As I explained to the Tiger 21 members that day, the critical question to ask yourself is: if you've already won the game, why are you still playing?

Needs versus Desires

One reason people continue to play a game they have already won is that they convert what were once desires (nice things to have, but not necessary to enjoy life) into needs. That increases the need to take risk. That causes an increase in the required equity allocation. And that can lead to problems when the risks show up, as they did in 1973–1974, 2000–2002, and again in 2007–2008.

Failing to consider the need to take risk is a mistake common to many wealthy people, especially those who became wealthy by taking large risks. However, the mistake of taking more risk than needed is not limited to the very wealthy. The question you need to ask yourself is how much money buys you happiness? Most people would be surprised to find that the figure is a lot less than they think.

Psychologists have found that once you have enough money to meet basic needs like food, shelter, and safety, incremental increases have little effect on your happiness. Once you have met those requirements, the good things in life (the really important things) are either free or cheap. For example, taking a walk in a park with your significant other, riding a bike, reading a book, playing bridge with friends, or playing with your children/grandchildren doesn't cost very much, if anything. Whether you drink a $10 bottle of wine or one that costs $100 or dine in a restaurant that costs $50 or $500 for dinner for two, both have the potential to make you happy.

Make sure that you have differentiated between needs and desires and carefully considered your marginal utility of wealth when developing your investment policy statement, so that you can determine if those desires are worth the incremental risks you will have to accept. Knowing when you have enough is one of the keys to playing the winner's game in both life and investing.

Hopefully, you will find the following tale helpful when you consider the issue of what's enough.

Pascal's Wager

Pascal's wager is a suggestion posed by the French philosopher Blaise Pascal that even though the existence of God cannot be determined through reason, a person should wager as though God exists—because the consequences of being wrong with each belief are very different. As author William Bernstein points out: "If a supreme being doesn't exist, then all the devout has lost is the opportunity to fornicate, imbibe, and skip a lot of dull church services. But if God does exist, then the atheist roasts eternally in hell."[4]

Those who have already achieved sufficient wealth to support a quality lifestyle face a similar wager. They can choose to either focus on the preservation of capital by having a low allocation to risky assets like equities, or they can choose to try to accumulate even more wealth by having a large allocation to risky assets. While it is likely that a high allocation will result in greater wealth, that outcome is not a certainty. And the consequences of going from rich to poor are intolerable for most people.

The bottom line is that the *consequences of decisions must always dominate the probabilities of outcomes.* That is why the prudent strategy for investors who have reached the point where their marginal utility of wealth is low is to have their portfolios be dominated by high-quality fixed income assets. There are some risks that are just not worth taking.

If you are deciding on which side of Pascal's wager you want to be with your portfolio, I recommend that you consider this important insight from author Nassim Nicholas Taleb:

> One cannot judge a performance in any given field (war, politics, medicine, investments) by the results, but by the costs of the alternative (i.e., if history played out in a different way). Such substitute courses of events are called *alternative histories*. Clearly the quality of a decision cannot be solely judged based on its outcome, but such a point seems to be voiced only by people who fail (those who succeed attribute their success to the quality of their decision).[5]

Conclusion

Victor Hugo was a French poet, playwright, and author, best known for *Les Miserables* and *The Hunchback of Notre Dame*. He was also a human rights activist who stated: "There is one thing stronger than all the armies of the world, and that is an idea whose time has come."

Despite the armies aligned against passive investing as the winning strategy, it is an idea whose time has come. Nothing Wall Street or the financial media can do will stop the trend away from active investing.

Arthur Schopenhauer was a German philosopher known for his clarity of thought. He had this to say about great ideas: "All great ideas go through three stages. In the first stage they are ridiculed. In the second stage they are strongly opposed. In the third stage they are considered to be self-evident."

The conventional wisdom on investing has been that the markets are inefficient, and smart people, working diligently, can, after the costs of their efforts, persistently exploit mispricings and deliver alpha. However, as Nicholas Chamfort, an eighteenth-century French writer best known for his wit noted: "There are well-dressed foolish ideas just as there are well-dressed fools."

The fact that something is conventional wisdom doesn't make it right. At one time, both "the Earth is flat" and "the Earth is the center of the universe" were conventional wisdom. In other words, even if millions of people believe a foolish thing, it doesn't make it less foolish. Active management as the winner's game is a foolish idea no matter how many people believe it or how fervent their belief. If you have not yet been convinced, perhaps the following will do the trick.

The Yale Endowment Fund

A study on the performance of the public equity investments of the highly successful Yale Endowment found that the returns were largely explained by exposure to risk factors and not manager skill. The endowment's exposure to small-cap and value stocks provided excess returns over the Wilshire 5000 (the chosen benchmark). A similar result was found internationally. While the endowment beat its benchmark (MSCI EAFE Index), some of the outperformance was explained by exposure to emerging market stocks and the same Fama-French risk factors. In other words, the benchmarks were wrong.

The authors concluded that any disciplined investor with a high risk tolerance could largely replicate Yale's results using publicly available index funds and some degree of leverage. They added that they saw value in Yale's broad diversification across asset classes with relatively low correlation.[1]

The implication is striking: If Yale, with all of its resources, can't identify the future alpha generators, what are the odds you can do so?

As Schopenhauer noted about great ideas, *the idea of index-ing was initially ridiculed.* Edward C. Johnson III is the chairman of Fidelity Investments. Note what he said about indexing: "I can't believe that the great mass of investors are going to be satisfied with just receiving average returns. The name of the game is to be the best."[2]

The following is the typical stockbroker's pitch when con-fronted with an investor who asks about indexing as an invest-ment strategy: "If you index, you will get average rates of return. You don't want to be average, do you? We can help you do better." Both stockbrokers and Edward Johnson are appeal-ing to what seems to be the all-too-human need to be "better than average." They ridicule and oppose indexing because it is the loser's game for them. And, as you have learned, they confuse market returns (which is what indexing delivers) with average returns. As William Sharpe demonstrated, by accepting market returns, passive investors in aggregate must outperform active investors in aggregate. Listen once again to Jonathan Clements: "It's the big lie that, repeated often enough, is even-tually accepted as truth. You can beat the market. Trounce the averages. Outpace the index. Beat the Street. An entire indus-try stokes this fantasy."[3]

In a great irony, Fidelity is now one of the world's leading providers of index funds.

The Way to Win Is Not to Play

Girolamo Cardano was a sixteenth-century physician, math-ematician, and quintessential Renaissance man. He advised: "The greatest advantage from gambling comes from not play-ing at all."

Similarly, the only sure way to win the game of active investing is not to play. The winner's game is to accept market returns by investing in low-cost, tax-efficient, and passively managed funds. Paul Samuelson put it this way: "It is not easy to get rich in Las Vegas, at Churchill Downs, or at the local Merrill Lynch office."[4]

Wall Street knows that. However, they want to make sure you don't reach that conclusion. They need you to keep playing the loser's game of active investing because it is the winner's game for them. As author Ron Ross put it, "Wall Street does its best to follow W.C. Fields's advice: 'Never smarten up a chump.'"[5]

The Quest for the Holy Grail

We have come to the end of our quest. Hopefully, it has become self-evident that the Holy Grail of investing is available to each and every investor. There are only two requirements. First, give up the quest for alpha and accept market returns. As you have seen, by doing so you are virtually guaranteed to outperform the vast majority of individual and institutional investors, assuming you have the discipline to stay the course.

Second, you must stop paying attention to the "noise" of the market. Noise causes investors to make decisions that are likely to prove unproductive. Paraphrasing *Barron's* financial journalist Alan Abelson, investing for the long term and paying attention to the daily ups and downs of the market is like walking with a yo-yo and paying attention to the yo-yo instead of where you are going.[6] To help accomplish this objective, consider this advice from Richard Thaler, professor of behavioral finance:

> I have not looked at any of my holdings and don't intend to. I don't want to be tempted to jump because I think I'd be more likely to jump in the wrong direction than the right one. My advice has always been to choose a sensible diversified portfolio and stop reading the financial pages. I recommend the sports section.[7]

Thaler's advice echoes that of Warren Buffett: "We continue to make more money when snoring than when active."[8]

The Winner's Game

I hope you have reached the conclusion that passive management of your portfolio is the winning investment strategy. Even more importantly, it is the winner's game in life. Let me explain.

Passive investing may have the "disadvantage" of being boring. However, it guarantees that you receive market returns in a low-cost and tax-efficient manner if you have the discipline to adhere to your investment policy statement. It also frees you from spending any time at all watching CNBC, studying charts, following Internet discussion sites, and reading financial publications that are basically not much more than the equivalent of astrology. Instead, you can spend your time with your family, doing community service, reading a good book, or pursuing your favorite hobby.

The bottom line is that if you play the game of active investing and you are skillful or lucky enough to be one of the few winners, the price you may have paid is that you lost the game of life—having spent far more time on less important issues. No one I know has written on his or her tombstone, "I produced persistent alpha." However, passive investors not only are virtually guaranteed to outperform the vast majority of individual and institutional investors, the time they don't spend actively managing their portfolios gives them a greater chance to win the far more important game of life.

To conclude our journey together, I offer the following. Perhaps the most asked question I receive about market efficiency and passive investing goes something like this: "But how do you explain Warren Buffett?"

The answer is simple. I tell them if, when they look in the mirror, they see Warren Buffett, go ahead and seek the Holy Grail of alpha. If they don't, give up the quest and play the winner's game. I believe Buffett would offer the same advice. Here is what he had to say about active investing: "Our stay-put behavior reflects our view that the stock market serves as a relocation center at which money is moved from the active to the passive."[9]

Appendix A

Rules of Prudent Investing

While we search for the answers to the complex problem of how to live a longer life, there are simple solutions that can have a dramatic impact. For example, it would be hard to find better advice on living longer than do not smoke, drink alcohol in moderation, eat a hearty breakfast and a balanced diet, get at least a half hour of aerobic exercise three to four times a week, and buckle up before driving. The idea that complex problems can have simple solutions is not limited to the question of living a longer life.

I have spent over 35 years managing financial risks for two leading financial institutions as well as advising individuals and multinational corporations on the management of financial risks. Based on those experiences, I have compiled a list of rules that will give you the greatest chance of achieving your financial goals.

1. *Do not take more risk than you have the ability, willingness, or need to take.* Plans fail because investors take excessive risks. The risks unexpectedly show up, and investors with 30-year horizons can turn into investors with 30-day horizons. That leads to the abandonment of plans. When developing your plan, consider your horizon, stability of income, ability to tolerate losses, and the required rate of return.

2. *Never invest in any security unless you fully understand the nature of all of the risks.* If you cannot explain the risks to your friends, you should not invest. Fortunes have been lost because people did not understand the nature of the risks they were taking.

3. *The more complex the investment, the faster you should run away.* Complex products are designed to be sold, not bought. You can be sure the complexity is designed in favor of the issuer, not the investor. Investment bankers don't play Santa Claus providing you with higher returns because they like you.

4. *Risk and return are not necessarily related; risk and expected return are related.* If there were no risk, there would not be higher expected returns.

5. *If the security has a high yield, you can be sure the risks are high, even if you cannot see them.* The high yield is like the shiny apple with which the evil queen entices Snow White. Investors should never confuse yield with expected return. Snow White could not see the poison inside the apple. Similarly, investment risks may be hidden, but you can be sure they are there.

6. *A well-thought-out plan is the necessary condition for successful investing; the sufficient condition is having the discipline to stay the course, rebalance, and tax-loss harvest as needed.* Unfortunately, most investors have no written plan. And emotions such as greed and envy in bull markets and fear

and panic in bear markets, can cause even well-thought-out plans to be trashed.

7. *Having a well-thought-out investment plan is the necessary condition for achieving your financial goals. Integrating the investment plan into a well-thought-out estate, tax and risk management (insurance of all kinds) plan is the sufficient condition.* The best investment plans can fail due to events unrelated to financial markets. For example, the breadwinner dies without sufficient life insurance, there is an accident and there is insufficient liability coverage, or disability or long-term-care insurance is needed but is not in place.

8. *Do not treat the highly improbable as impossible, nor the highly likely as certain.* Investors assume that if their horizon is long enough, there is little to no risk. The result is that they take too much risk. Taking too much risk causes investors with long horizons to become short-term investors. Stocks are risky no matter the horizon. And remember, just because something has not happened doesn't mean it cannot or will not.

9. *The consequences of decisions should dominate the probability of outcomes.* We buy insurance against low-probability events (such as death) when the consequences of not having the insurance can be too great to accept. Similarly, investors should insure their portfolios (by having an appropriate amount of high-quality fixed income investments) against low-probability events when the consequences of not doing so can be too great to contemplate.

10. *The strategy to get rich is entirely different than the strategy to stay rich.* One gets rich by taking risks (or inheriting it). One stays rich by minimizing risks, diversifying, and not spending too much.

11. *The only thing worse than having to pay taxes is not having to pay them.* The "too many eggs in one basket" problem

often results from holding a large amount of stock with a low cost basis. Large fortunes have been lost because of the refusal to pay taxes.

12. *The safest port in a sea of uncertainty is diversification.* Portfolios should include appropriate allocations to the asset classes of large and small, value and growth, real estate, international developed markets, emerging markets, commodities, and high-quality bonds.

13. *Diversification is always working; sometimes you'll like the results, and sometimes you won't.* Diversification in the same asset class reduces risk without reducing expected returns. However, once you diversify beyond popular indices (such as the S&P 500), you will be faced with periods when a popular benchmark index outperforms your portfolio. The noise of the media will test your ability to adhere to your strategy. Remember, a strategy is either right or wrong before the fact.

14. *The prices of all equity and risky bond assets (such as high-yield bonds and emerging-market bonds) tend to fall during financial crises.* Your plan must account for this.

15. *Identifying a mispriced security is the necessary condition for outperforming the market; the sufficient condition is being able to exploit any mispricing after the expenses of the effort.* The "history books" are filled with investors that tried to exploit "mispricings," only to find that trading (and other) costs exceeded any benefits.

16. *Equity investing is a positive-sum game; expenses make outperforming the market a negative-sum game.* Risk-averse investors don't play negative-sum games. And most investors, probably including you, are risk averse. Use only low-cost, tax-efficient, and passively managed investments.

17. *Owning individual stocks and sector funds is more akin to speculating, not investing.* The market compensates investors for risks that cannot be diversified away, like the risk of investing in stocks versus bonds. Investors shouldn't expect

compensation for diversifiable risk—the unique risks related to owning one stock, or sector or country fund. Prudent investors only accept risk for which they are compensated with higher expected returns.

18. *Take your risks with equities.* The role of bonds is to provide the anchor to the portfolio, reducing overall portfolio risk to the appropriate level.

19. *Before acting on seemingly valuable information, ask yourself why you believe that information is not already incorporated into prices.* Only *incremental* insight has value. Capturing *incremental* insight is difficult because there are so many smart, highly motivated analysts doing the same research. If you hear recommendations on CNBC or from your broker or read them in *Barron's*, the market already knows the information it is based on. It has no value.

20. *The four most dangerous investment words are "This time it's different."* Getting caught up in the mania of the "new thing" is why "the surest way to create a small fortune is to start out with a large one" is a cliché.

21. *The market can remain irrational longer than you can remain solvent.* Bubbles do occur. However, investors should never attempt to short them because, while bubbles eventually burst, they can grow larger and last longer than investor resources.

22. *If it sounds too good to be true, it is.* When money meets experience, the experience gets the money and the money gets the experience. The only free lunch in investing is diversification.

23. *Never work with a commission-based adviser.* Commissions create the potential for biased advice.

24. *Work only with advisers who will provide a fiduciary standard of care.* That is the best way to be sure the advice provided is in your best interest. There is no reason not to insist on a fiduciary standard.

25. *Separate the services of financial adviser, money manager, custodian, and trustee.* This minimizes the risk of fraud.

26. *Since we live in a world of cloudy crystal balls, a strategy is either right or wrong before we know the outcome.* In general, lucky fools do not have any idea they are lucky. Even well-thought-out plans can fail because risks that were accepted occur. And risks that were avoided because the consequences of their materializing would be too great to accept may not occur.

27. *Hope is not an investment strategy.* Base your decisions on the evidence from peer-reviewed academic journals.

28. *Keep a diary of your predictions about the market.* After a while, you will conclude that you should not act on your "insights."

29. *There is nothing new in investing, just the investment history you don't know.* The knowledge of financial history will enable you to anticipate risks and incorporate them into your plan.

30. *Good advice does not have to be expensive; but bad advice always costs you dearly, no matter how little you pay for it.* Smart people don't choose the cheapest doctor or the cheapest CPA. Costs matter; but it is the value added relative to the cost of the advice that ultimately matters.

Appendix B

Doing It Yourself

Warren Buffett said: "Investing is simple, but not easy."[1] Investing is simple. To be successful, you only need to follow the 30 prudent rules of investing laid out in Appendix A. However, it is not easy because there's actually more to investing. Writing in the Winter 2003 edition of the online journal *The Efficient Frontier*, author William Bernstein laid out these four additional requirements for investors to be able to succeed on their own:[2]

- "An *interest* in investing. It's no different from cooking, gardening, or parenting. If you don't enjoy it, you'll do a lousy job. Most people enjoy finance about as much as Carmela Soprano enjoys her husband's concept of marital fidelity."
- "The horsepower to do the math . . . The Discounted Dividend Model, or at least the Gordon Equation? Geometric versus arithmetic return? Standard deviation? *Correlation*, for God's sake? Fuggedaboudit!"

- "The knowledge base—Fama, French, Malkiel, Thaler, Bogle, Shiller—all seven decades of evidence-based finance back to Cowles. Plus, the 'database' itself—a working knowledge of financial history, from the South Seas Bubble to Yahoo!"
- "The emotional discipline to execute faithfully, come hell, high water, or Bob Prechter. Mr. Bogle makes it sound almost easy: 'Stay the course.' Alas, it is not."

Bernstein noted:

> An optimist might guess a 30 percent success rate on each count, in which case 1 percent of the population can make all four. Perhaps I overstate the case. After all, these four abilities are not entirely independent: If you're smart enough, it's more likely you'll be interested in finance and be driven to delve into the appropriate finance literature. But even if true, more than a little luck is involved. Head down to the personal-finance section of your local Barnes and Noble, and you're more likely to run into Suze Orman than Jack Bogle. You'll need a telescope to find the really important stuff.

Bernstein concluded: "I wish I had a nickel for every smart, savvy, and motivated financial type I've met who simply could not execute."

This last point is extremely important. Investing is simple but not easy because, while staying the course is easy when everything is going well, when bear markets inevitably arrive, the best-laid plans can end up in the trash heap of emotions. In other words, it is much easier to establish a good investment plan than to adhere to it. Peter Lynch advised: "Whatever method you use to pick stocks or stock mutual funds, your ultimate success or failure will depend on your ability to ignore the worries of the world long enough to allow your investments to succeed. It isn't the head, but the stomach that determines the fate of the stockpicker."[3]

There are some individuals who can do it all on their own. If you think you are one of them, make sure you meet the four requirements laid out by William Bernstein. And be sure you are not falling prey to the all-too-common human tendency toward overconfidence.

Some individuals recognize that they do not have the knowledge, the interest, or the discipline required to do it on their own. They also recognize that a good financial adviser can add value in many ways. There are also individuals who would rather have someone else focus on financial matters so they can focus their attention on the more important things in their lives. They know that even if they have the skills to do it themselves, the time spent on financial matters is time not spent with family and friends, doing community service, and so on. And they place a greater value on that time than on the cost of an adviser. They might also hire an adviser because doing so would allow them to spend more time doing more of the work at which they are experts (such as being a doctor or lawyer), and for which they get paid more than they pay in advisory fees.

A good financial adviser can add value in many ways. For example:

- Developing an investment plan that provides the greatest chance of achieving your financial goals without exceeding your ability, willingness, or need to take risk.
- Integrating your investment plan into an overall estate, tax, and risk management plan.
- Helping you act like a postage stamp—sticking to your plan until you reach your financial goal.

Unfortunately, it is far too easy for someone to become a financial or investment adviser. The requirements are few and the tests far too easy. In the case of most Wall Street firms, training is mostly sales and compliance oriented with little emphasis on investment knowledge. If it weren't so dangerous, it would be humorous that advertisements for brokers typically include the phrase "no experience necessary."

So how do you find a competent adviser whom you can trust to act in your best interests? When interviewing a potential financial adviser, you should require them to make the following 11 commitments to you. Doing so will give you the greatest chance of avoiding conflicts of interest and the greatest chance of achieving your financial goals.

1. The firm should be able to demonstrate that its guiding principle is to provide investment adviser services that are in the client's best interests.

2. The firm follows a fiduciary standard of care. A fiduciary standard is often considered the highest legal duty that one party can have to another. This differs from the suitability standard present in many brokerage firms. That standard requires only that a product or service be suitable; it does not have to be in the investor's best interest.

3. The firm serves as a fee-only adviser—avoiding the conflicts that commission-based compensation can create. With commission-based compensation, it can be difficult to know if the investment or product recommended by the adviser is the one that is best for you or the one that generates greater compensation for the adviser.

4. All potential conflicts are fully disclosed.

5. Advice is based on the latest academic research, not on opinions.

6. The firm is client-centric—advisers focus on delivering sound advice and targeted solutions. The only requirement they have in offering particular solutions is whether the client's best interests will be served. The firm is focused on providing advice, not products.

7. Advisers deliver a high level of personal attention and develop strong personal relationships, and because no one can be an expert on all subjects, clients benefit from a team of professionals to help them make sound financial decisions.

8. Advisers invest their personal assets (including the firm's profit-sharing/retirement plan) based on the same set of investment principles and in the same or comparable securities they recommend to their clients.

9. They develop investment plans that are integrated with estate, tax, and risk management (insurance) plans. The overall plans are tailored to each client's unique personal situation.

10. Their advice is goal oriented—evaluating each decision not in isolation but in terms of its impact on the likelihood of success of the *overall* plan.

11. Comprehensive wealth management services are provided by individuals with Certified Financial Planner (CFP), Personal Financial Specialist (PFS), or other comparable designations.

Because the cost of bad advice can be so high, you should also perform a thorough due diligence on the firm. That due diligence should not only include requiring the adviser to make the aforementioned 11 commitments to you, but it should also include a careful review of form ADV—a disclosure document setting forth information about the adviser, including the investment strategy, fee schedules, conflicts of interest, regulatory incidents, and so on. And, finally, you should consult other professionals (CPAs, attorneys) in the area, as well as current clients, to get *independent* references on the firm. Careful due diligence will minimize the risk of having to make expensive repairs.

Notes

Chapter 1

1. Mark Carhart, Jennifer N. Carpenter, Anthony W. Lynch, and David K. Musto, "Mutual Fund Survivorship," *Review of Financial Studies*, Winter 2002.

2. Mark Carhart, "On Persistence in Mutual Fund Performance," *Journal of Finance*, March 1997.

3. Christopher B. Philips and Francis M. Kinnery Jr., "Mutual Fund Ratings and Future Performance," Vanguard Institute, February 2010.

4. "The Dangers of Over-Diversification," investopedia.com/articles/01/051601.asp (accessed June 2010).

5. Travis Sapp and Xuemin (Sterling) Yan, "Security Concentrations and Active Fund Management: Do Focused Funds Offer Superior Performance?" *Financial Review* 43 (2008).

6. Christopher R. Blake, Edwin J. Elton, and Martin J. Gruber, "The Performance of Bond Mutual Funds," *Journal of Business*, July 1993.

7. Jaclyn Fierman and Kathleen Smyth, "The Coming Investor Revolt," *Fortune,* Oct. 31, 1994.

8. Marlena I. Lee, "Is There Skill among Active Bond Managers?" December 2009.

9. Russel Kinnel, "Time to Clear Out the Dead Wood," *Morningstar FundInvestor,* December 2004.

10. Bradford Cornell, "Luck, Skill and Investment Performance," *Journal of Portfolio Management,* Winter 2009.

11. Eugene F. Fama and Kenneth R. French, "Luck versus Skill in the Cross Section of Mutual Fund Returns," June 2009.

12. Thomas Gilovich, R. P. Vallone, and Amos Tversky, "The Hot Hand in Basketball: On the Misperception of Random Sequences." *Cognitive Psychology* 17: 295–314.

13. Burton G. Malkiel, *A Random Walk Down Wall Street* (New York: W. W. Norton & Company, 1996).

14. Marc Gunther, "Yale's $8 Billion Man," *Yale Alumni Magazine,* July/August 2005.

15. David Swensen, *Unconventional Success* (New York: Free Press, 2005).

16. John Bogle, *Common Sense on Mutual Funds* (New York: John Wiley & Sons, 1999).

17. Ralph Wanger, *A Zebra in Lion Country* (New York: Simon & Schuster, 1997).

18. Kirk Kazanjian, *Wizards of Wall Street* (Paramus, NJ: Prentice Hall, 2000).

19. W. Scott Simon, *Index Mutual Funds* (Camarillo, CA: Namborn, 1998).

20. Russel Kinnel, "Expenses Trend Down, but Total Fees Keep Rising," *Morningstar Advisor,* April 2005.

21. Bethany McLean, "The Skeptic's Guide to Mutual Funds," *Fortune,* March 15, 1999.

22. David Whitford, "Where Have All the Geniuses Gone?" *Fortune,* October 11, 1999.

23. Bethany McLean.

24. Ibid.

25. Jonathan Clements, "How You Can Pick a Winning Stock Fund," *Wall Street Journal,* December 22, 1998.

26. "An Interview with Morningstar Research Director John Rekenthaler," *In the Vanguard*, Autumn 2000.

27. Tom Lauricella, "A Tough Bear Market Knocks 'Value' Managers Off Pedestals," *Wall Street Journal*, October 2, 2008.

28. Benjamin Graham and Jason Zweig, *The Intelligent Investor* (New York: HarperCollins, 2003).

29. Jonathan Clements, "Only Fools Believe in Managed Funds," *Wall Street Journal*, September 15, 2002.

Chapter 2

1. Rob Bauer, Rik Frehen, Hurber Lum, and Roger Otten, "The Performance of U.S. Pension Plans," February 2007.

2. Amit Goyal and Sunil Wahal, "The Selection and Termination of Investment Management Firms by Plan Sponsors," May 2005.

3. T. Daniel Coggin and Charles A. Trzcinka, "A Panel Study of Equity Pension Fund Manager Style Performance," *Journal of Investing*, Summer 2000.

4. Edwin J. Elton, Martin J. Gruber, and Christopher R. Blake, "Participant Reaction and the Performance of Funds Offered by 401(k) Plans," May 2006.

5. Barry Burr, "Big Caps Are Too Efficient," *Pension & Investments*, June 26, 2000.

6. "The 1997 Pension Olympics," *Institutional Investor*, May 1997.

7. Philip Halpern, Nancy Calkins, and Tom Ruggels, "Does the Emperor Wear Clothes or Not?" *Financial Analysts Journal*, July/August 1996.

Chapter 3

1. Stephen J. Brown, William N. Goetzmann, and Roger G. Ibbotson, "Offshore Hedge Funds: Survival and Performance, 1989–95," *Journal of Business*, January 1999: 98.

2. David Dremen, "Las Vegas on Wall Street," *Forbes*, January 11, 1999.

3. Roger G. Ibbotson and Peng Chen, "The A, B, Cs of Hedge Funds: Alphas, Betas, and Costs," Working Paper (September 2006): 5, 13.

168 NOTES

4. Gregory Zuckerman, "Hedge Funds Weather Stormy Year," *Wall Street Journal*, January 2, 2008.

5. Harry M. Kat, "10 Things that Investors Should Know about Hedge Funds," *Journal of Wealth Management,* Spring 2003: 7.

6. Burton G. Malkiel and Atanu Saha, "Hedge Funds: Risk and Return," *Financial Analysts Journal,* November/December 2005.

7. Greg Gregoriou, "Hedge Fund Survival Lifetimes," *Journal of Asset Management,* December 2002: 249.

8. Ken Brown, "New Study Snips Away at Hedge Funds," *Wall Street Journal*, February 22, 2001.

9. Carl Ackermann, Richard McEnally, and David Ravenscraft, "The Performance of Hedge Funds: Risk, Return and Incentives," *Journal of Finance,* June 1999.

10. Malkiel and Saha.

11. Nolke Posthuma and Pieter Jelle van der Sluis, "A Reality Check on Hedge Fund Returns," Working Paper (July 2003): 20, 25.

12. David Swensen, *Unconventional Success* (New York: Free Press, 2005), 126.

13. Craig Karmin, "Yale's Investor Keeps Playbook," *Wall Street Journal*, January 13, 2009.

14. Lynn O'Shaughnessy, "Brain Trust," *Bloomberg Wealth Manager,* November 2002.

15. Laurence Kotlikoff and Scott Burns, *Spend 'til the End* (New York: Simon & Schuster, 2008), 39.

16. Gary Weiss, *Wall Street versus America* (New York: Penguin Group, 2006), 110.

17. Ibid., 111.

Chapter 4

1. Ventureeconomics.com.

2. Ibid.

3. Steve Kaplan and Antoinette Schoar, "Private Equity Performance: Returns, Persistence and Capital Flows," *Journal of Finance,* August 2005: 1791.

4. John H. Cochrane, "The Risk and Return of Venture Capital," *Journal of Financial Economics,* January 2005: 4.

5. Tobias J. Moskowitz and Annette Vissing-Jorgensen, "The Returns to Entrepreneurial Investment: A Private Equity Premium Puzzle?" *American Economic Review,* September 2002: 746.

6. Ludovic Phalippou and Oliver Gottschalg, "The Performance of Private Equity Funds," Working Paper (April 2007).

7. Cochrane, 3, 10, 30, 32.

8. Ibid., 20.

9. Peng Chen, Gary T. Baierl, and Paul D. Kaplan, "Venture Capital and Its Role in Strategic Asset Allocation," *Journal of Portfolio Management,* Winter 2002: 2, 4.

10. Phalippou and Gottschalg.

11. David Swensen, *Unconventional Success* (New York: Free Press, 2005), 92–93.

Chapter 5

1. Brad Barber and Terrance Odean, "Boys Will Be Boys: Gender, Overconfidence and Common Stock Investment," *Quarterly Journal of Economics,* February 2001.

2. Terrance Odean, "Do Investors Trade Too Much?" *American Economic Review,* December 1999.

3. Wilber G. Lewellen, Ronald C. Lease, and Gary G. Schlarbaum, "Patterns of Investor Strategy and Behavior among Individual Investors," *Journal of Business* 50 (1977): 296–333.

4. Brad Barber and Terrance Odean, "Too Many Cooks Spoil the Profit: Investment Club Performance," *Financial Analysts Journal,* January–February 2000.

5. Russel Kinnel, "Mind the Gap," *Morningstar FundInvestor,* July 2005.

6. Richard Haig, "Did You Do As Well As Your Fund," Morningstar.com, August 7, 2009.

7. John Bogle, "The Yawning Gap between Fund Returns and Shareholder Returns," *Journal of Indexes,* May/June 2008.

8. Jason Zweig, "What Fund Investors Really Need to Know," *Money,* June 2002.

9. David Swensen, *Unconventional Success* (New York: Free Press, 2005), 203.

10. E. S. Browning, "All the Wrong Moves," *Wall Street Journal*, May 16, 1997.

11. Brad Barber and Terrance Odean, "Too Many Cooks Spoil the Profit."

12. Gary Belsky and Thomas Gilovich, *Why Smart People Make Big Money Mistakes—and How to Correct Them: Lessons from the New Science of Behavioral Economics* (New York: Simon & Schuster, 1999).

13. Daniel Kahneman, "Hard Wired," *Dow Jones Asset Management*, November–December 1998.

14. Jonathan Fuerbringer, "Why Both Bulls and Bears Can Act So Bird-Brained," *New York Times*, March 30, 1997.

15. David Barboza, "A Wrestler for Market Freedom," *New York Times*, February 21, 1999.

16. Holman Jenkins, "Business World: Why 'Restitution' Is a Bad Idea," *Wall Street Journal,* November 27, 2002.

17. Jonathan Clements, *25 Myths You've Got to Avoid If You Want to Manage Your Money Right* (New York: Simon & Schuster, 1998), 55.

18. Henry Blodget, "The Trouble with CNBC and Smart Money and . . . " Slate.com, November 11, 2004.

19. Robert Barker, "It's Tough to Find Fund Whizzes," *BusinessWeek*, December 17, 2001.

Chapter 6

1. Prithviraj Banerjee, Vaneesha R. Boney, and Colby Wright, "Behavioral Finance: Are the Disciples Profiting from the Doctrine?" *Journal of Investing,* Winter 2008.

2. Fullerthaler.com.

3. Markus Glaser and Martin Weber, "Why Inexperienced Investors Do Not Learn: They Don't Know Their Past Portfolio Performance," July 2007.

4. Jon E. Hilsenrath, "As Two Economists Debate Markets, the Tide Shifts," *Wall Street Journal*, October 18, 2004.

5. Burton Malkiel, "Are Markets Efficient—Yes, Even if They Make Errors," *Wall Street Journal*, December 28, 2000.

Chapter 7

1. Mark Rubinstein, "Rational Markets: Yes or No? The Affirmative Case," *Financial Analysts Journal,* May–June 2001.

2. Ron Ross, *The Unbeatable Market* (Eureka, CA: Optimum Press, 2002), 57.

3. Mark Rubenstein.

4. Raymond Fazzi, "Going Their Own Way," *Financial Advisor* (March 2001).

5. Peter Bernstein, *Against the Gods* (New York: John Wiley & Sons, 1996).

6. Richard Oppel, "The Index Monster in Your Closet," *New York Times*, October 10, 1999.

7. Carole Gould, "It's Gnawing at Your Fund, and Now It Has a Gauge," *New York Times*, July 11, 1999.

8. Roger Edelen, Richard Evans, and Gregory B. Kadlec, "Scale Effects in Mutual Fund Performance: The Role of Trading Costs," March 17, 2007.

9. W. Scott Simon, *Index Mutual Funds* (Camarillo, CA: Namborn, 1998), 208.

10. Speech by John Bogle, Three Challenges of Investing, Client Conference, Boston, MA, October 21, 2001.

11. Jonathan B. Berk, "Five Myths of Active Management," *Journal of Portfolio Management*, Spring 2005.

12. Ibid.

13. Jeffrey A. Busse, Amit Goyal, and Sunil Wahal, "Performance Persistence in Institutional Investment Management," *Journal of Finance,* April 2010.

14. William Sherden, *The Fortune Sellers* (New York: John Wiley & Sons, 1998).

15. Michael W. McCracken, "How Accurate Are Forecasts in a Recession," Federal Reserve Bank of St. Louis, *Economic Synopsis*, no. 9 (2009).

16. William Sherden.

17. Ibid.

18. Philip E. Tetlock, *Expert Political Judgment: How Good Is It? How Can We Know?* (Princeton, NJ: Princeton University Press, 2005).

19. J. Scott Armstrong, "The Seer-Sucker Theory: The Value of Experts in Forecasting," *Technology Review*, June/July 1980: 16–24.

20. Ron Ross, *The Unbeatable Market,* (Eureka, CA: Optimum Press, 2002).

21. Richard M. Ennis, "Are Active Management Fees Too High?" *Financial Analysts Journal,* September 2005.

22. Mark Hebner, *Index Funds,* (Irvine, CA: IFA Publishing, 2007).

23. William Sherden.

24. Stephen Gould, *Full House* (Chatsworth, CA: Harmony, 1996), 32.

25. Perry Mehrling, *Fisher Black and the Revolutionary Idea of Finance* (Hoboken, NJ: John Wiley & Sons, 2005), 138.

26. Gene Epstein, "Prizing Caution," *Barron's,* June 2, 1997.

27. Peter Bernstein and Frank Fabozzi, eds., *Streetwise,* paperback ed. (Princeton, NJ: Princeton University Press, 1998), 3.

28. Mark Sellers, "Could Stocks Still Be Undervalued?," *Morningstar,* February 18, 2004.

29. Jeremy Siegel, *The Future for Investors* (New York: Crown Business Publishers, 2005).

30. David Altany, "New Jobs for the Number Crunchers," *Industry Week,* April 20, 1992: 76.

31. Robert Lenzner, "Bearish on America," *Forbes,* July 19, 1993.

32. Lawrence Armour and Joe McGowan, "A Superstar's Global View," *Fortune,* December 23, 1996.

33. Fred Bleakley, "What Recession? A Forecast Change Moves This Economist to Top of List," *Wall Street Journal,* January 2, 1997.

34. Gretchen Morgenson, "In Uncertain Times, Put Surprise to Work," *New York Times,* January 14, 2001.

35. "Shopping Spree: The Dow Gains 4.7% as Bargain Hunters Swarm Into Stocks," *Wall Street Journal,* October 29, 1997.

36. Jason Zweig, *Your Money or Your Brain* (New York: Simon & Schuster, 2007), 76.

37. "John Liscio, 51, Bond Newsletter Publisher," *New York Times,* December 9, 2000.

38. Scott Burns, "Fidelity's Return Policy," *Los Angeles Times,* July 22, 1997.

39. Ben S. Bernanke, address at the 2009 Commencement of the Boston College School of Law, Newton, MA, May 22, 2009.

Chapter 8

1. Dwight Lee and James Verbrugge, "The Efficient Market Theory Thrives on Criticism," *Journal of Applied Corporate Finance,* Spring 1996.

2. Rob Kozlowski, "BlackRock Takes the Lead in Indexing," *Pensions & Investments,* September 20, 2009.

3. Tara Kalwarski, "Time to Take Action?" *BusinessWeek*, September 7, 2009.

4. *2008 Investment Company Fact Book* (Washington, DC: Investment Company Institute, 2008), 20, 36.

5. *2010 Investment Company Fact Book* (Washington, DC: Investment Company Institute, 2010), 33.

Chapter 9

1. Paul Farrell, "Where Are the Customers' Yachts?," *MarketWatch,* November 27, 2006.

2. Gregory Baer and Gary Gensler, *The Great Mutual Fund Trap* (New York: Broadway Books, 2002), 20.

3. Ibid., 22.

4. Dan Ariely, *Predictably Irrational* (New York: HarperCollins, 2009), 227.

5. Derek DeCloet, "Shift in CIBC Focus Puts Whizz in Closet," *Financial Post,* December 5, 2001.

6. Ted Lux, *Exposing the Wheel Spin on Wall Street* (Bloomington, IN: IUniverse, 2000), 40.

7. John Dorfman, "Market Timing Also Stumps Many Pros," *Wall Street Journal,* January 30, 1997.

8. Leah Nathans Spiro, "'Flat Fee' Accounts: Read the Fine Print," *BusinessWeek,* July 14, 1997.

9. John Merrill, *Outperforming the Market* (New York: McGraw-Hill, 1998).

10. Christopher Buckley, "IRS, Mon Amour," *Forbes,* March 2010.

11. Peter Bernstein, *Against the Gods* (New York: John Wiley & Sons, 1996), 219.

12. Steve Forbes, Excerpt from presentation at The Anderson School, University of California, Los Angeles, April 15, 2003.

13. "Confessions of a Former Mutual Funds Reporter," *Fortune*, April 26, 1999.

14. Caroline Baum, "Punditry Is Always and Everywhere the Same," *Bloomberg*, February 23, 2000.

15. Scott Burns, "Decide on Index, Avoid Decisions," *Dallas Morning News*, August 10, 2005.

16. William Sharpe, "The Arithmetic of Active Management," *Financial Analysts Journal*, January/February 1991: 7–9.

17. Ibid.

18. "Low-Turnover Funds Outperform Their Active-Trading Rivals," *St. Louis Post Dispatch*, August 12, 1997.

19. John Bogle, *Common Sense on Mutual Funds* (New York: John Wiley & Sons, 1999), 286.

20. Kathryn Welling, "By the Numbers: Wall Street's Fees and the Market Are Both Too High, Says Manager," *Barron's,* June 15, 1998.

21. Russ Wermers, "Mutual Fund Performance: An Empirical Decomposition into Stock-Picking Talent, Style, Transaction Costs, and Expenses," *Journal of Finance,* August 2000.

22. Kenneth R. French, "The Costs of Active Investing," April 2008.

23. Mark Hebner, *Index Funds* (Newport Beach, CA: IFA Publishing, 2007), 125.

24. Jonathan Clements, "How You Can Pick a Winning Stock Fund," *Wall Street Journal*, December 22, 1998.

25. "Is There Life After Babe Ruth?" *Barron's*, April 2. 1990.

26. Berkshire Hathaway Annual Report, 1996.

27. Andy Serwer, "The Oracle of Everything," *Fortune*, November 11, 2002.

28. Michael Lewis, "The Evolution of an Investor," *Conde Naste Portfolio*, December 2007.

Chapter 10

1. FutureMetrics, December 2006.

2. Jonathan Clements, "Mutual-Fund Investing Is a Good Plan, but Don't Wed Yourself to the S&P 500," *Wall Street Journal*, June 17, 1997.

3. John Bogle, "Fixing a Broken Financial System," *Vanguard*, February 12, 2009.

4. Jonathan Clements and William J. Bernstein, *The Little Book of Main Street Money* (Hoboken, NJ: John Wiley & Sons, 2009), xvii.

5. Nassim Nicholas Taleb, *Fooled by Randomness* (New York: Random House, 2008), 22.

Conclusion

1. Peter Mladina and Jeffery Coyle, "Yale's Endowment Returns: Manager Skill or Risk Exposure," *Journal of Wealth Management*, Summer 2010.

2. Ben Warwick, *Searching for Alpha* (New York: John Wiley & Sons, 2000), 17.

3. Jonathan Clements, *25 Myths You've Got to Avoid* (New York: Simon & Schuster, 1998), 54.

4. Peter Bernstein, *Capital Ideas* (New York: Free Press, 1991), 17.

5. Ron Ross, *The Unbeatable Market* (Eureka, CA: Optimum Press, 2002), 11.

6. Scott West and Mitch Anthony, *Storyselling for Financial Advisors* (Chicago: Dearborn Financial Publishing, 2000), 213.

7. Lauren Young, "Where the Pros Are Putting Their Own Money," *BusinessWeek*, October 2, 2008.

8. Berkshire Hathaway Annual Report, 1996.

9. Berkshire Hathaway Annual Report, 1991.

Appendix B

1. Clifford Asness, "Rubble Logic: What Did We Learn From the Great Stock Market Bubble?," *Financial Analysts Journal*, November/December 2005: 51.

2. William Bernstein, "The Probability of Success," *Efficient Frontier*, Winter 2003.

3. Peter Lynch, *Beating the Street* (New York: Fireside, 1993).

Sources of Data

The following are the sources for data contained in the text:

Standard & Poor's for data on the S&P 500 Index and the S&P GSCI. Used with permission.

Kenneth R. French and the Center for Research in Security Prices at the University of Chicago for data on the various Fama-French series. Used with permission.

Morgan Stanley for data on the MSCI indexes. Used with permission.

Barclays for data on the Barclays Capital Intermediate Government/ Credit Index. Used with permission.

About the Author

Larry E. Swedroe is principal and director of research for The Buckingham Family of Financial Services, which includes Buckingham Asset Management and BAM Advisor Services. Buckingham Asset Management manages more than $2.7 billion in assets for individuals, businesses, trusts, not-for-profits, and retirement plans. BAM Advisor Services provides turnkey asset management services for more than 120 registered investment adviser firms and manages or administers more than $9.8 billion in assets. Swedroe has held executive-level positions at Prudential Home Mortgage, Citicorp, and CBS. He speaks frequently at financial conferences throughout the year and writes the blog "Wise Investing" for CBS MoneyWatch.com.

Index